In the Arms of Inup

The extraordinary story of a Guatemalan survivor
and his quest for healing from trauma

Eve Mills Allen

HARP Publishing The
People's Press
Clydesdale, Nova Scotia
Canada

Juan Jeremias Tecu Quisque, Fredericton, New Brunswick

Photo Credit: Mayte Mercedes Tecu

In the Arms of Inup

The extraordinary story of a Guatemalan survivor
and his quest for healing from trauma

Copyright 2020 © Eve Allen

Published in Canada by HARP the People's Press,
216 Clydesdale Road, Clydesdale, Nova Scotia, B2G 2K9
www.harppublishing.ca

All rights reserved. No part of this book may be used or reproduced
in any manner without written permission from the publishers

Information about purchasing this book can be obtained from the publishers:

harppeoplespress@gmail.com

tel 902-863-0396

Catalogue-in-Publication data is on file with Library of Congress Canada

ISBN: 978-0-9938295-6-7

Printed in Canada by Rapido Books

Cover Artist: Jody Claus

Graphic Design: Cathy Lin

Author Photo: Sasha Laagland

Praise for *In the Arms of Inup*

This book takes you into the heart of the healing process of storytelling between a compassionate listener and a refugee survivor of horrific cruelty and injustice. The safe space created by unconditional acceptance and positive regard informs us about how an empathic approach can respond to the needs of trauma survivors.

Jeremias' story points to the lack of culturally sensitive mental health services that recognize the burden of carrying untold stories of trauma. A lack of compassionate social services for survivors of atrocious injustices will only serve to send the survivors underground and reinforce fear and shame. In order to support the successful integration of refugees into our Canadian society, we must rise to the task of developing trauma-based and culturally sensitive mental health services.

- Sandra deVink, retired social work professor at St. Thomas University (1985-2014)

Eve Mills Allen is an exceptional storyteller. She has triumphed through great adversity in her own life to emerge with newfound vision, heart and understanding. What she has to share will benefit many.

- Kenneth J. Harvey, author/filmmaker

This book is a "must read" for mental health professionals working in the field of trauma with refugees and newcomers to Canada. It is a poignant reminder of the importance of creating a safe space in order to hear the story being shared.

- Dr. Helen Massfeller PhD, L.Psych. CCC, professor, University of New Brunswick

TABLE OF CONTENTS

Foreword	8
Introduction	10
1. In the Beginning	16
2. In the Arms of Inup	21
3. Escape	31
4. New Home for the Refugees	40
5. Father's Unexpected Return	52
6. Balancing Family and Work	62
7. Connecting with BTS	74
8. Exhumations	77
9. Danger at Every Turn	85
10. Baby Amanda Jasmine	93
11. Hope in the Midst of Danger	97
12. A New World	105
13. A Child's Perspective: Leaving Guatemala	108
14. A New Beginning	111
15. Settling in for Oscar	120
16. Fitting In	123

17. Hints of Racism	133
18. Breaking the Silence in Canada	135
19. First Trip Back to Guatemala	138
20. Grim Reality	143
21. Medicating the Demons	147
22. Spiritual Connection	155
23. Peso: A Gift from a Mam Grandmother	164
24. Back to Guatemala: Between Two Worlds	172
25. A Small Bit of Justice	184
26. Full Circle	188
27. Where to Go from Here	202
28. Closure?	207
29. Jeremias On Services for Survivors	209
30. The Therapist/Writer/Friend of Jeremias	213
Bibliography	217
Acknowledgements	218

Foreword

This marvelous book is all about breaking silences and their transformative potential. First and foremost, it is an intimate portrait of a survivor of the Guatemalan genocide against Mayan peoples. Seeking to heal from unbearable experiences, Jeremias chooses to break the silence within that is constraining his life in immense pain and suffering. With incredible courage and determination, he seeks out a helper who will share this journey with him. Jeremias eventually finds Eve and over six years, he reveals his memories in a profoundly honest and moving process of telling his story. Rare enough in itself to hear a survivor speak, the story could easily end there. But there is so much more to learn from this book.

In his struggle to find help, we learn from Jeremias how wholly inadequate our mental health system is in supporting people traumatized by war, institutionalized violence, and genocide. We learn how everyday practices of the system itself work against creating the safety and trust needed to do the work. By challenging these conventional counselling practices, Jeremias and his counsellor are renaming the problem, and saying what needs to be said on behalf of those who cannot. But once again, we are not left there. In an inspired turn, Eve shares with us her own experience as counsellor/friend as she accompanies Jeremias on his journey and writes his story. Accompaniment is a theme that weaves throughout the book and provides a new way to conceptualize the therapeutic process.

Breaking the silence in the Guatemala of the 1980s, 1990s, and even today can still mean the difference between life and death. Jeremias' story also tells the story of his people, the horrors of the genocide they endured during "la violencia" and today as they seek justice for their communities. Through his telling we learn of the spiritual and cultural practices that sustain the survivors. Ultimately, we learn that the only "cure" for survivors of collective trauma is to stop the wars, violence, and genocide in the first place. In receiving this story, we as readers now share in that responsibility.

Suzanne Dudziak PhD
Fredericton, New Brunswick
September 2020

Dr. Dudziak was engaged in solidarity work with Central America (including Guatemala) for several decades as a researcher and activist with the Latin American Working Group (LAWG). She recently retired from teaching in the School of Social Work at St. Thomas University. She is currently a member of Breaking the Silence—Fredericton (BTS).

Introduction

Juan Jeremias Tecu Quisque lived in a tiny village area of Rabinal in Guatemala in the 1960s. He was a child when Civil War began in his country. This war in Guatemala raged on from 1960 to 1996. The widespread killing of the Mayan people, innocent victims, deemed it a genocide. Most still refer to it as a massacre. I met him as an adult in Canada while facilitating a therapeutic writing course. As a professional psychotherapist and writer, I often use the creative arts like storytelling as part of the healing process. It was after this course that Jeremias asked me to help him tell his story.

Jeremias is one of the victims who survived. This story —the story of one family's survival, led by an 11-year-old boy —is a snapshot of those times, and a look at the mental health risks of bringing survivors to an unfamiliar country unsure of how to meet their needs. At Jeremias' request, some names in this story have been changed.

Guatemala is a country in Central America bordered by Mexico to the north and west, the Pacific Ocean to the southwest and Belize to the northeast. It is filled with striking geographical contrasts and natural beauty. It reaches from the Cuchamatán Mountains in the western highlands to the coastlines on the

Caribbean Sea and the Pacific Ocean. It is also dotted with thick forests, Mayan ruins, lakes, volcanoes, orchids and exotic birds and animals. Its indigenous population, the Maya, make up about half of the population. Mayan languages are spoken alongside Spanish, the official tongue.

But the magnificence of this country stands in harsh contrast to its bloody past and troubled present. The biggest blight on the landscape is the mines. Silver, nickel, gold, zinc and lead mines rip holes throughout the country, destroying water supplies and land. They are strongly supported by companies in the United States and Canada. Even in 1960, Canada and the United States were heavily invested in nickel mining in Guatemala.

A land reform law, known as the Agrarian Reform Law (Decree 900), passed in 1952. Introduced by President Jacobo Árbenz Guzmán, it redistributed unused lands to local peasants, compensating landowners with government bonds. The Indigenous Mayan peoples were major beneficiaries of the decree and they were given an opportunity finally to find autonomy as they cultivated the land given to them. This angered major landowners and the United States, who had vested interests in this area. In 1954, a coup d'état deposed Árbenz and instigated the decades of Civil War to follow.

In 1960, the political climate was volatile and life for many indigenous peoples was forever changed. It was the beginning of 36 years of horror the government called a *civil war*. The indigenous population knew it as *genocide*—a massacre that killed approximately 200,000 Guatemalan civilians.

Kidnappings, unimaginable, extreme torture, rape and destruction of complete villages were the trademarks of this time, particularly for the Mayan people. Even though a Peace Accord was signed in 1996, slaughter continues though less visibly.

On May 13, 2013, CNN announced: *Former Guatemalan dictator Efrain Rios Montt was found guilty of the genocide of more than 1,700 indigenous Ixil Mayans during his 1982-83 rule. A three-judge panel issued the verdict Friday, one day after the conclusion of the trial. The court sentenced Rios Montt, 86, to 80 years in prison.*

When Rios Montt became president, human rights violations had already prompted the United States to cut off aid to the Guatemalan government. But a political scandal in the United States in the 1990s revealed that in fact the Central Intelligence Agency continued to provide money to Guatemalan military intelligence sources for years during the civil war.

Now-declassified secret CIA cables indicate the United States had knowledge of the atrocities being committed against the Ixil Mayans but did little about them. Then-U.S. President Ronald Reagan went as far as to say that Rios Montt was being given a "bum rap" by critics. At the same time, the United States was backing other strongmen in Latin America against leftists.

But the conviction was overturned by the constitutional court, which argued Rios Montt had been denied due process. A court official said that the judges were busy with other cases in 2014, and would resume the trial in January 2015, but the lawyer claimed his client was mentally incompetent, and Rios Montt was eventually kept on house arrest, and the case continued. In November 2016, another announcement came forth: *Four members of the army's elite troop, which executed the massacre, were already condemned to over 6,000 years in prison five years ago. One lieutenant was sentenced to over 5,000 years and two others accused of participating in the massacre are detained in the United States, where they are serving a sentence for lying to obtain U.S. citizenship.*

On February 26, 2016, Lieutenant Coronel Esteelmer Reyes was sentenced to 120 years in prison for crimes against humanity, including sexual violence, sexual slavery and domestic slavery, as well as murder. Former Military Commissioner Heriberto Valdez Asij was convicted of crimes against humanity, including sexual violence, sexual slavery, domestic slavery, and the disappearances of seven men. He was sentenced to 240 years in prison. In December 2016, a decision by the Inter-American Court of Human Rights found the Guatemalan state guilty of crimes against humanity for the massacres in Chichupac, Rabinal in the 1980s.

These are media accounts reporting the small tokens of justice. They can never make up for the devastation suffered by so many, including the children—children, like Jeremias Tecu, who escaped the massacre but who, even as adults, cannot escape the memories.

In *Guatemala: Never Again!*—The official report of the Human Rights Office, Archdiocese of Guatemala—there are many accounts of the violence against women: soldiers committed mass rapes during massacres or detentions of women. Rape was part of the war machinery and women were frequently sexually assaulted in front of their families. One case reported, Case 11724, perpetrator Xecojom, Nebaj, Quiche, 1980, recounts: *One day I was able to escape and, while hidden, I saw a woman. They shot her and she fell. All the soldiers left their packs and dragged her like a dog to the riverbank. They raped and killed her. Also, a helicopter that was lying overhead landed, and they all did the same thing to her.*

It is hard to understand how such horrendous acts of violence could dominate this beautiful land and its gentle people. Rabinal, Baja Verapaz, sits in the valley of the Sierra Chuacas Mountains, the central part of Guatemala, just a few hours north of Guatemala City. The highland municipality of Rabinal, home of the Maya Achí people, was one of the regions brutally targeted by the scorched earth policy of the early 1980s. It has been estimated that more than 5,000 people were executed by the Guatemalan military and its death squads in a two-year period; most of the victims were Maya Achí.

Eve Mills Allen
Moncton, New Brunswick Canada
October 15, 2020

In the Arms of Inup

The extraordinary story of a Guatemalan survivor and his quest for healing from trauma

1

In the Beginning

Jeremias bows his head before the monument in Rabinal, tears coursing down his cheeks, as memories slash through his brain. Here are the names of those who were senselessly slaughtered—his relatives, his friends, his people. Although it has been 35 years since he escaped this massacre, the pictures of that time turn steadily off and on as if someone were working a flashlight in the night—vividly bright, then black. But nothing can extinguish the crying or the screams, and, even in the dark, blood is still red.

Jeremias Tecu was only eleven when he became a man. The disappearance of his father and two older brothers left him, as the oldest male in the family, no choice but to step quickly into the adult role. The smell of acrid smoke winding its tentacles around decomposing flesh, and the sight of scattered body parts, sealed this premature appointment and impelled him to step up and take responsibility. To save his remaining family, Jeremias bravely directed his mother and younger siblings, one only a month old, to hide in the roots of the huge Inup, a tree greatly feared by all Mayan children.

Jeremias lived in La Ceiba near the small town of Rabinal, a Maya Achí village in Guatemala. He loved his home and his family and, even though he worked very hard, the work was something he enjoyed, something that made him feel connected to the earth around him and to his family. The massacre began in his village in 1981, taking with it his carefree spirit. It was Inup that saved his life, but it could in no way shelter his mind from the images that would become seared on his brain for a lifetime.

Jeremias' father, Felix, was a community leader and a tireless worker for the Catholic Church, but although his connection to the Church was strong, he also believed in his Mayan traditions and ceremonies. He was known by the locals as a Mayan priest. He was also the president of the small co-op for his village, a peaceful protester who used teaching to help his people survive through the genocide that raged on for more than twenty years. He taught people how to sow new kinds of vegetables that could be seeded and used for exchanges in other villages. He encouraged them to stay united and strong in the face of growing threats to their homes and personal safety.

Born in the tiny village of Pichec, Jeremias' mother, Pedrina Quisque Ic, was relatively tall by Mayan standards, a slender, attractive woman who dressed in bright colors. She was only 15 when she married 18-year-old Felix, Jeremias' father. She protested and told her father she did not want to marry. She pointed out she had not yet become a woman, but there was no arguing with her father. Felix was a hard worker and well respected. He came from a modestly successful family and had lots of land and two houses. She knew she had no choice, so she accepted her destiny. But after they were married, Pedrina, who was never afraid to speak her mind, teased her husband often about being taller than him. Jeremias recalls how his mother typically loved to dress in colorful traditional clothing. Red was always the dominant color, and multicolored strings would sometimes be woven into her hair.

"She was beautiful, and she was not afraid of anything," Jeremias says. "She had the spirit of a warrior and she loved her family and her country. She was more angry than afraid when the invasions began."

By 1980, the military had begun to select those they would exterminate among the Mayan peoples. They targeted those who did not want to surrender their homes or land, to make way for government expansion that favored the foreign nickel-mining companies from the United States and Canada. People like Felix were often branded as "revolutionaries" or "communists." By the age of ten, Jeremias had already seen how suspected "revolutionists" were tortured and killed by the soldiers representing the interests of the country's leader. It is a time he does not like to remember. Seeing people he knew hanging from their necks on trees, after being beaten or cut and sometimes raped, caused him to pretend it must not be real, just so he could function. His normal world transformed, and even at that young age he knew these grotesque images were warnings to keep him from disobeying the people in control. Pedrina's two brothers and one of her two sisters were all killed during this time.

On a Sunday after church in August 1981, only a few days before the birth of his youngest child, Felix Tecu went missing. His family questioned everyone they saw, but no one knew what had happened. The word in the marketplace was that the soldiers had been asking for him.

"After a few days went by, we knew he must have been kidnapped," says Jeremias. "We missed him, but we had no time to do anything about it. We needed to survive and keep going. There was so much work to do, so we did it and just hoped maybe he would return."

The following month the situation became even more desperate. The soldiers were now burning homes and selecting people from his community to torture as a warning to everyone else that they were in charge. On September 13, 1981, the soldiers turned their focus on the Tecu family. Jeremias and his cousin, also only ten years old at the time, hid in the bushes as the military surrounded his uncle Antonio, his uncle's wife, and their other four children. Two of the children, young teenage girls, were made to strip and dance for the soldiers as their terrified family watched in humiliation. The soldiers then raped the girls and the mother before slowly and deliberately torturing the father and his sons by cutting them with a knife. In the end, all were killed and left for others to see. Jeremias and his cousin could not believe it was real. It was as if the world in which they still lived was completely separate from the one where all the killing took place. They felt nothing. But telling it now, so many years later in a different country, Jeremias can no longer suppress the feelings locked away for so long.

"It was beyond emotion," Jeremias says to me, with tears in his eyes. "I felt like my mind and body were not together. I saw it all, but it was like I was somewhere else. I felt nothing. Not even fear."

2

In the Arms of Inup

As I take another sip of my tea, I look at Jeremias and marvel at the miracle that brought him all the way from Central America to Atlantic Canada. It may have been close to three decades since he had been a child fighting for survival in the middle of the Guatemalan massacre, but he carried the torturous memories with him every day. His search for help with the mental anguish was what caused our paths to cross in the first place. I was offering a new way to help, and he was desperate to find something to alleviate his emotional pain. So far his quest for appropriate mental health services in his new country had brought only frustration.

He looks troubled, so I ask if he would like to wrap up our time together, but he shakes his head. He has asked me, a writer and mental health therapist, to write his story, to help him work through the process, and he is determined to do it. With a deep breath, he begins to relate his incredible story to me:

"I can't forget that night. It is like a horror movie, not real but too real at the same time. My cousin was in shock, I think. He lost his whole family that night. He stayed with us after that for a while, but when he became a teenager, he joined the guerrillas to fight the soldiers, and they killed him too. But he stayed with us right after they killed his family.

"That day was supposed to be a normal day. We were celebrating our new member of the family Tecu, our brother, Felix. There was a lot to celebrate, even though we were aware of dangers in other villages. My father had disappeared without a trace shortly after my mother became pregnant, but we just kept doing what we needed to do to survive. No one could tell us what happened to him, so we stopped talking about it. But when the baby was born, my mother gave him my father's name, Felix.

"My three oldest siblings were living away, two in Guatemala City and one in Antigua, Guatemala, a little town not far from Guatemala City. The three of them decided to travel to Rabinal in the department of Baja Verapaz. Our Departments are like provinces in Canada. It was a trip that took eight hours on the bus used by most of the people for transportation. They were coming to meet and celebrate my brother.

"My two brothers were so happy because finally, after four sisters and only three brothers in our family at the time, with the new baby we were equal in gender—four boys and four girls. There were now eight of us—at least for a while.

"The day of their arrival in Rabinal was not a good day for our villages. Someone destroyed some important bridges that connected our communities, so that first night with everyone together sleeping at home was a mix of feelings. There was happiness, but also a lot of fear. I remember my brother, Oscar, who was 17 at the time, telling us he was really afraid.

He looked very sad and he said we should all pray. Oscar planned to be a priest. My oldest brother, Simeon, who was 25 at that time, was braver and tried to help him.

'Do not worry, man,' he told Oscar. 'Remember you just have to worry if you are part of the guerrillas or a helper. Then you will definitely be in trouble with our governments, but we do not have to worry. I know how the government works, because I was a soldier and I'm trained to stand for my country. I'm with you; nothing will happen.'

"On the second day, we went to Rabinal town, about 45 minutes away by walking, to shop. My three younger sisters, Alba, Olivia and Virginia, stayed at home. First, we went to the Catholic Church for the Sunday service, then we had lunch together under an avocado tree in front of the church. It was a sunny, beautiful day as we ate our tortillas and *boxboles* (a filling cooked in flour and wrapped in pumpkin leaves). We finished our meal around 1 pm, then we divided ourselves into two groups. My mother, the baby brother, my oldest sister, Odilia, who was 18 at the time, and I went home to la Ceiba Village to relax. We sometimes sat under the tree we call Inup in the daytime. It was a popular place in the afternoon, but no one went near it at night.

"My two brothers went to city hall to do some ID diligences for my brother Oscar. He needed to get official ID to use for preparing to enter the priesthood. But something was different that day. It wasn't the same Sunday as we usually have with people after church happy and more relaxed—laughing and visiting with other family members. No one was laughing that day. People were sad and running around. I saw fear in their faces.

"That day was the last time I saw my older brothers. At home, we were waiting for my brothers almost all night. When they never came back home, on the second day my oldest sister had to go back to Antigua, Guatemala, but my mother, my baby brother and me, decided to go around visiting my uncles, aunts, relatives, friends, to see if my brothers were there or if anyone had seen them. But no one had seen them. We found out a lot of people had been killed. I saw so many bodies, so my mother and I walked around among the dead and tried to identify if my brothers were there or not. We went to many places with no luck. We despaired that my brothers were dead, but we could not find them.

"My mother decided, on the second day of the search, to go to the military base in Rabinal Baja Verapaz town to ask if they had seen my brothers. I did not want her to go. I had to take care of my baby brother. She was incarcerated, but they let her go the next day. I saw bruises all over her face. Even now, I'm not sure if she was raped by the military; my mother never talked about it. During that week we noticed many strangers walking in our villages. The military were destroying houses, killing domestic animals. They raped girls of any age in front of their parents, brothers, community, including my relatives. When I realized that, I worried about my three little sisters and mother."

Jeremias tries hard to block out these kinds of memories, and not to speculate on what happened to his mother during her detention and beatings by soldiers. He does recall asking the priest on more than one occasion to save her. Relentlessly, the pictures of the torture and dead bodies kept trying to capture his mind, but he fought hard to concentrate only on how to survive. Some memories need to be extinguished as quickly as possible. In part, Jeremias did this by pretending it was not real. It was just a bad dream. Others remained safely concealed in compartments, ever present yet contained most of the time; otherwise the trauma would take over. Jeremias says he simply ran out of compartments when he got older. As a boy, focusing only on survival kept him motivated.

He takes a deep breath and continues: "I remember, I was crying, and I told Mom, 'I don't want to die! Tonight, we will hide … We will go and sleep under Inup,' and I pointed to the big tree. I was more afraid of the soldiers than the legend. That night, my uncle and his family were butchered, and my little cousin came with us."

"Why were you afraid of the tree?" I ask, allowing Jeremias to pause and turn his thoughts to something else. I couldn't imagine reliving this horror. "Do you want to stop?"

Jeremias smiles, but the tears still dominate his dark eyes. His eyes, the colour of the black coffee he is drinking, reach out for my understanding.

"I can't," he says. "It has to be told. It has to come out from inside of me. When it comes out, it might not hurt so much."

Never had I heard the true value of therapeutic writing summed up so succinctly in anything I'd studied or read about this subject.

"Yes, my friend, it has to come out of you," I say as I pat his arm. "But not all at once; let's talk about the legend first."

Inup, also known as *la Ceiba*, was the most sacred tree for the ancient Maya, and according to Maya mythology, it was the symbol of the universe. The tree signifies a route of communication between the three levels of earth. Its roots are said to reach down into the underworld, its trunk represents the middle world where the humans live, and its canopy of branches arched high in the sky symbolizes the upper world.

All Mayan Achi children have heard the story of Inup. It is Guatemala's national tree and some tower as high as 100 feet or more. The clefts and branches at the top can measure up to 150 feet across and the large, long capsules that appear as the fruit of the tree contain cotton fibres. It is these fibres that make up a portion of the legend. Jeremias heard the legend many times from his maternal grandmother. He is ready to talk about something less heart-wrenching for a while.

He smiles as he begins: "*La Ceiba* (Inup) is important in our culture. We have a lot of legends and stories, and one the most famous and fascinating is the legend of the Inup. Our elders told us that Inup comes alive at night and everything else, like monkeys and other creatures, play around and they all have a type of string or cotton that they use to cover the entire Inup at night. These monkeys and other creatures taking care of

Inup don't allow others to see or pass under Inup at nighttime to protect the sacred tree. We were never to go there at night. The legend says that if any human being passes under the tree at night he or she will disappear forever and never come back in life.

"As a Mayan Achi child, we were very respectful of our grandmother, and obviously we never did anything against what she had been teaching us. In the daytime it was different. I remember I would go with my cousins and other relatives at the school break time after having fun swimming and then we would pick some mangos and oranges and go under the huge branches of the Inup. It was safe in the daylight. We played hide and seek. We had a lot of fun, but it was still a little bit scary because we remembered that always before the sun goes down, we had to run, and everybody must be home before night comes. If we were still there at night, the legend says no one would ever find us again. All of us feared Inup at night.

"I was a very happy child until I reached ten years old, because after that we saw a lot of dead people, from a very young age to adult. They killed them at night and some of them were hanging from their necks, tortured, raped, to warn all of us to do what they wanted. I did not feel like a child after that." For young Jeremias, his fear of Inup paled in comparison to the horrors existing on the night he first ran to the sacred tree for shelter. The stage had been set. The gigantic roots became ceilings of tiny compartments worn into the earth by the path of the long-departed river. It was these compartments that then became the tiny safe houses for families on this fateful night and many more to come.

Jeremias explains: "My friends were going place to place with me to see other people from our neighboring villages. People were not talking about it; on this morning all was silent. No dogs barked; even the rooster was completely silent. It was the beginning of something so upsetting and sad it tore our world apart. The unity of our community, brotherhood, and sisterhood had been divided. No one even trusted another member of the family. Anyone could break under enough threats or torture and help the enemy.

"There was too much anger. People, like my brothers and father, were disappearing. They said the killing was our fault. Just to be a student or community leader, any type of community participation—it was labeled communism, guerrilla activity or revolution. There was the danger of revenge if someone thought you were with on the wrong side. I knew we had to hide in order to survive. At nighttime they would attack, I just felt it. Inup was the only place to hide and even though I was scared, that is where I took my family. I was only eleven, but I was in charge now. They killed my uncle Antonio, my father's youngest brother. They tortured him and killed his children and his wife. The other son escaped to Inup with us. We no longer feared the legend, and we soon found out just how much this tree actually protected us.

"Inup became a mother for us. It looked like the branches were our mother's arms, and its trunk was like our mother's body which protected us. At night we were completely silent and just like the legend said, we were invisible to outsiders. We heard the bombs, the sounds of the gunshots, people screaming; we knew houses were being burned. At the time, my mother and my three little sisters and baby brother were with me, also an aunt and her three children. My uncle couldn't make it. He was captured by the soldiers, and later that week they killed him among other community leaders in Rabinal.

"From a distance, Inup was a big tree. Perhaps in the eyes of many people it was just a simple tree, but for us it was a mother who protected us. The first night we ran for its protection, that was the night they burned my uncle's home to the ground. We did that for 12 days, from 6:30 pm until around 5:30 am before the sun rose, so the soldiers would think everything was normal. We did not want to be attacked at night or our home set on fire with us in it. The tree hid us, but it did not hurt us. It kept us safe. We passed the time by taking time to sleep, while the adults were taking turns to guard the place. We all put together dry leaves from the tree and used them as a bed as we hid in the large hollowed out spaces made by the giant roots.

"Every morning we heard lots of different birds singing, so we knew when it was the right time to leave. We did not really have to say who should leave first. It just happened. The only thing we knew was to leave the place in small groups, so no one would notice that we were hiding under that tree. During our 13th night, our house was burned and looted. They took anything of value. That night was our last night in *la ceiba—Inup*. My mother still wanted to stay, but I begged her to go. My mother did not want to leave her home village. She wanted to find her sons. She wondered where her husband was, and she wanted to stay on the piece of earth that had been her home for so long. But there was nothing left—nothing but ashes and decaying bodies, so many body parts.

"We decided to walk somewhere safe, but with no idea where to go. Many people of all ages were walking to escape from persecution. We did not know where to go, but one thing we had in common is that we didn't want to die and have the same luck as many of our relatives, friends, brothers, sisters, parents. *'I do not want to die,'* I reminded her. So my mother, baby brother, and three little sisters followed me into the mountains. For us, the Tecu family, it took around 45 days walking in the mountains and forest. We did not have food, and we ate what we found in the trees and the river, in this journey of escaping from persecution. But that is another story."

3

Escape

Jeremias searched for his brothers with his mother, baby brother and three sisters for three days before leaving. They tried to avoid looking at the dead bodies left to rot on the sides of the roads and on pathways leading to where their homes once stood. The air was rancid and the mood of the survivors increasingly fearful. Some moved like zombies, as if life had already been removed from their bodies. Others ran about quickly, paranoid that they would be seen and killed, trusting no one, not even family members. Jeremias constantly fought with his mother to leave before they were all killed. She clung fiercely to her few belongings, and the remnants of hope that she would find her sons. That was until the day Jeremias decided to leave without her and take his sisters with him. The children took nothing with them. They wore the same clothing they had on for the past week, no shoes or sandals.

"I just started walking," he says. "My mother didn't give in at first. I told my sisters to follow me, and they did. We didn't know where to go, but I knew it was now or never," he explains. "We knew it was dangerous, but that moment was our only opportunity to live."

It was very early in the morning. The full moon was still out. Jeremias took comfort from its beauty and felt encouraged by the light that allowed him to manoeuvre easier in the dark. When his mother realized her children were really leaving, she gave in reluctantly and followed with the baby, and what she could carry with her. Jeremias led the way, walking on a road he knew would lead to another village. They walked until they found a safe area to hide, and even along this escape route they found more bodies.

"I thought the killing was just in our community," Jeremias says. "I thought walking away would bring peace, but what we saw brought even more fear, and determination to escape."

The tired group walked until they could walk no more. When they stopped it was no longer dark. They met other people along the way who were also looking for a safe place. These people often brought warnings that the military were coming from a certain direction, so Jeremias and his family changed paths many times, sometimes walking through the mountainous area where the thick foliage could hide them better.

"We just walked and kept in mind we needed to get out of there," he says. "We tried not to see what was there, so much death and destruction. But I never felt any fear. I felt frozen inside, numb. I kept telling myself this is not really happening."

The family walked mostly in silence. Sometimes off in a distance, they could hear shooting or dogs barking. But even most of the dogs were silent. Many of them were slaughtered too. As they approached each new community, Jeremias hoped he would find some place untouched by the horror of the massacre. Each time, he was disappointed.

"We could hear people crying as we approached many of the communities," he says. "No one was spared the anger of the military."

In the journey to a place of safety where they could find a new home, the surviving villagers along the way would sometimes provide small amounts of food, or a chance to sleep in safety. Sometimes they had wooden matches to give them, so they could make their own fires along the way. Everyone knew or had heard about Jeremias' father. Felix had been highly regarded among the Mayan people, so they treated the Tecu family with the same degree of respect. Jeremias learned from the survivors that they had experienced the same things as his community only a couple of weeks before. But most of the trip was spent in the mountains so they would not be seen, and most of the time they survived by eating only roots or leaves. The hunger never left, and Jeremias says it was especially hard on his sisters.

"My sisters would ask for food because they were so hungry, and I felt so bad I could not get more for them," he says. "Mostly we ate roots and some fruit. Once we found bananas. We even cooked some green bananas at night, being careful that no one could see us. There were streams along the way, and we drank water from them."

There were many dangerous things in the mountains, but Jeremias only worried about the military.

"Ordinarily, I would be afraid of the snakes," he says. "The snakes slept in the same place we slept at night and they were big, but I did not even think about that. There were coyotes, panthers, mountain lions, even poisonous spiders and scorpions, but we did not get hurt. My mother and I took turns watching while the others slept."

The days and nights with little food, water or sleep and the exertion of constantly walking, often in rough terrain, eventually took its toll.

"We were all becoming sick," Jeremias recalls. "It was cold at night too. We looked for plants that were used as traditional medicines to help us. There is a plant for stomachache, fever, and headaches. There is a kind of flower for this, another one to protect us from too many mosquito bites. We just ate the blossoms. We were not sure if they were even the right ones, but we had no choice."

Traveling with a young baby added to the hardships faced by the family. Pedrina brought only T-shirts, which needed cleaning once or twice a day. She had been nursing the baby but, through sickness and exhaustion, her milk quickly dried up. Luckily, in one of the villages along the way she was able to get powdered milk. For as long as it lasted, this was the baby's main diet.

"That was a big problem," Jeremias explains. "It was not easy to get powdered milk and the baby was sick, too, from the cold and too little food. He cried a lot, but Mom tried to keep him quiet by suckling him. That would make him more upset because there was no milk. It was hard to keep him quiet when we tried to hide. That was always a worry, but after a while he didn't cry so much. I think he was giving up, too. That is why I tried even harder to lead my family to some place where we could have a home again."

Jeremias' sister, Alba, was not quite seven years old. She grew tired more easily, and often begged to stop walking. Stopping was not an option in Jeremias' young mind.

"We were so tired we couldn't talk much," he recalls. "Many times, the girls asked where we were going, or when would we find somewhere safe to stop. I had no answers, so sometimes I just did not answer. Mom kept talking about her sons. She was worried about how she would ever make it back to our village, to what she left behind. All I worried about was completing this journey without anyone being killed, or worse."

Before he escaped to the mountainous region, Jeremias also struggled with the decision to leave everything that was familiar to him. But as he walked with his mother, baby brother and three little sisters on paths littered with the remains of their dead neighbours and relatives, he decided the unknown could be no worse than this alien landscape that had swallowed his childhood home. It was surreal, like a bad dream. But he also knew death was everywhere, and he knew he did not want to die. More than that, even though he was still young he sensed the killers would return. His baby brother would never survive, and he did not want his mother and sisters to suffer the humiliating torture he had already witnessed reserved for the females. He knew they had to leave and if his mother would not come, he was determined to protect his sisters. He would do his best to guard them in the forest. It was their only hope.

He continues: "We just kept walking. When we approached a village, I would go ahead to make sure the military was not still in the community before we stopped there. One evening as we were resting, I watched a spider build its nest. Before that, I used to feel afraid of these big spiders, but this time I felt it had a message for me. It was part of me, my relation. As I watched, I thought about its strength, how it never gave up. I knew even if something hurt the web, it would just rebuild. That seemed to give me strength too. After all, even at eleven, wasn't I stronger than a spider?"

Jeremias sighs as he finishes his story. Even more than 30 years later, recounting these memories is a painful exercise for him. Sometimes during his storytelling, even I wanted to stop, to think and write about something else. I often cried with him and wondered if this was really helping him. I considered abandoning the project and suggested to Jeremias that maybe he should stop, but it was at these times that Jeremias pushed on harder, insisting we continue. Ironically, it was those times when he did not show strong emotion that he required longer breaks—days, even months—before he was ready to start telling his story again. I learned a great deal about how to work with post-traumatic stress disorder (PTSD) by following his lead. There is one incident that stands out particularly in Jeremias' mind.

"One time, we had to run because we came by a community where they were doing massacres. We met villagers running away, two of them tortured and bleeding. We were so scared we left the baby. We had to hide him in some bushes and pray he would not cry. He did not cry much anymore. But after it was over and we met up with each other, we each thought the other had picked him up. We had to spread out and we made plans to meet up, but then we realized little Felix was missing. We had been hiding for two or three hours. Mom told me not to go back, that they had probably already killed him, but I could not do that. Even though I knew it could still be dangerous, I went to look, and I found him. He was laying there playing. He was not scared at all, but I was more scared than I had been in a long time. I cried as I grabbed him and ran back. It was a miracle. My mother cried too, and from then on she carried him all the time."

Jeremias said his mother argued with him after that, saying they should go back to Rabinal. She thought maybe things had changed since they had been gone so many days. Jeremias firmly said "No." He explained that his mother estimated they had been traveling for probably about 45 days. She based this in part on the moon, remembering it had been full when they left and there had been another one since. It was not long after that that they arrived in Coban, Alta Verapaz, a place where they knew they could find help. They needed to get to the outskirts of Guatemala City, still many hours away, where many of the wandering displaced people were setting up camps. But first, they needed to find help from the Catholic sisters.

Jeremias left his family in a safe hiding place outside the area where his mother told him he could find the nuns who knew his father. He travelled approximately three-quarters of an hour to the house where they lived, his heart pounding with each step. Now he was totally alone and still responsible for the welfare of his family. He was not sure what kind of reception he would find at the door of the sisters who had befriended his father so long ago. When he saw the house, he gathered every bit of courage he could find and walked to the door.

He recalls: "First thing, I didn't want to show my fear to the sister who opened the door, but she could see how bad it was. She asked in Spanish if I was hungry, but I didn't understand much Spanish. I only spoke Achi. I tried to explain about who my father was and how my father and brothers had disappeared, and that we had been walking in the forest for several days. I finally broke down and she fed me and asked, 'Where is your mom?' Then she took a jeep and set out to get my family.

"That was the beginning of another journey. When we arrived at the place where my family was hiding, we stayed there until it was becoming dark. Then the sister dressed us up in clothes she had brought with her and put us in a minivan. Along the way were checkpoints. It was very dangerous, but she pretended we were sick and had us lying down and she took us to Guatemala City. The soldiers stopped her several times. She told them she had dying people and was taking them to hospital. She said it might be something contagious, she didn't know. She even had an intravenous pole hooked up to one of my sisters to make it look more real.

"It was a rough, bumpy drive that took nine hours. The lack of food, sleep and safety took its toll. We really did get sick and most of us vomited. We felt sad and tired, confused, a mix of feelings, but it was the safest we'd been in a long time, so hope began to grow as the sister took us to Guatemala City to the home of a priest she knew. He was from Belgium, and right away he welcomed us and opened his space to us. He even had a secret hiding place in case the soldiers came. Most people escaping had no home to go to, but we were very blessed to find a temporary home with this kind man right away."

4 New Home for the Refugees

Casas de Carton	*Cardboard Houses*

Que triste se oye la iluvia
en los techos de cartón
Que triste vive mi gente
en las casas de cartón.

How sad it is to hear the rain
on the cardboard roofs.
How my people live sadly
in the cardboard houses.

Viene bajando el obrero
casi arrastrando sus pasos
por el peso del sufrir
Mira que mucho ha sufrido
Mira que pesa el sufrir.

The worker descends
almost dragging his steps
from the weight of suffering.
See how much he has been suffering
See the weight of suffering.

Arriba deja la mujer preñada
abajo está la ciudad
y se pierde en su maraña.
Hoy es lo mismo que ayer,
es un mundo sin mañana.

Above he leaves the pregnant woman,
below is the city,
and he becomes lost in the maze.
Today is the same as yesterday,
it's a world without a tomorrow.

Niños color de mi tierra
con sus mismas cicatrices
millonarios de lombrices,
y por eso…
Que triste viven los niños
en las casas de cartón.

Children the colour of my earth
with their own scars
millionaires of worms
and so …
How the children live sadly
in the cardboard houses.

Que alegres viven los perros,
casa del explotador.

How happily the dogs live
in the exploiter's house.

Usted no lo va a creer
pero hay escuelas de perros
y les dan educación
pa' que no muerdan los diarios,
pero el patron
hace años muchos años
que está mordiendo al obrero.

You are not going to believe it
but there are dog schools
that give them education.
so they don't bite the news reporters
but the pattern has been set for
many years, that is, biting the worker.

Que triste se oye la Iluvia
en los techos de cartón
Que lejos pasa la esperanza
en las casas de cartón

How sad the rain is
on the cardboard roofs.
How far hope goes
in cardboard houses.

Jeremias sings this song to me. He says it speaks about the experience of the refugees. Most people fleeing from the villages and towns for safety came to the outskirts of Guatemala City and lived in shelters made from plastic bags and cardboard cartons. This settlement (*Tierra Nueva*) was near the dump, with no running water or bathrooms of any kind until the people built a latrine. Water was purchased in containers from a truck and it cost two quetzals, which at that time was equivalent to fifty cents American. The people earned money in whatever way they could. Mothers washed clothing for the richer people. The men and boys were sometimes lucky enough to get an odd job helping at a construction site. It was always the hardest labour that fell to them. The adolescents (and even younger) often went to work in the sweat shops run by larger corporations. Some turned to prostitution.

"Some worked seven days a week without even a bathroom break during their long days," Jeremias says. "There were children as young as ten who worked in these sweat shops. They tested the girls to make sure they were not pregnant and could do the work. If they were pregnant, they would be rejected."

Prostitution claimed more victims. Now predators roamed the camp. But Jeremias and his mother and small siblings were more fortunate than many. The priest, Padre Adrian Bashancen Ostan, was willing to help them because of his knowledge of Jeremias' father's work for the Catholic Church, and he allowed them to live at his house. He moved into an adjoining one that was used for theology students but was empty at the time. Even though Jeremias and his family needed to hide most of the time and could not be seen outside the house in the daytime for several months, they were grateful for a place to live. Still, it was a big adjustment for everyone, especially his mother, and there was never enough food to extinguish the constant hunger pains.

The priest gave them a home with a small kitchen and stove to use and two metal pots, but Jeremias' mother wouldn't use them. She wanted clay pots like the ones she used at home.

"She said the food tasted like leather in the other pots," Jeremias remembers. "Even though life was hard, we laughed about this."

She also wanted to cook outside, so as soon as it was safe enough, Jeremias helped to construct an outdoor kitchen. He wanted to make his mother happy. Besides the priest's house, there were three other small houses connected to the main one, all designated for theology students. There was also a chapel and a small farm on the same site with pigs and chickens. Jeremias recalls one of the times the army came looking for anyone they could accuse of being a guerrilla:

"The priest saw them coming, so he hid us in a cellar. This house had a kind of root cellar that was like a small basement. Houses in Guatemala do not usually have basements, so the soldiers did not even think to look under the floor. There was a door in the floor where we climbed down and then the priest covered it with a mat. The army went through the houses around us and took some of the animals from the farm with them. Some of them they butchered and left as a warning to us. We were scared but they never found us. Once my mother dug a hole and hid the few books in our house, so they could not give a clue we were there. We could not leave our house for six months to make sure we would be safe."

Many people were kidnapped from the camp when they were approached by the army and could not answer questions, especially youth 18-19 years old. Many were tortured and killed, shot without mercy just because they couldn't understand the language. Sometimes they were tortured to try to make them confess they were involved with the guerrillas. Anyone who was close to the church would be killed. When Jeremias was finally able to venture out into the new community, he was shocked by the size of the neighborhood and the suffering of his fellow refugees—the internal settlers who were also displaced from their homes.

"Rabinal was two or three streets only," he tells me. "We had less than 7,000 people. The refugee camp was a much larger area that held at least 25,000 people made up of all these new communities. Many people had heard this would be a place of safety, so they came to escape and the numbers on the outskirts of Guatemala City kept growing. In the poorer settlement area, a few people managed to get tents, but some still lived in shelters made from cardboard boxes. People were hungry and had little clothing. Everywhere there was pain and despair. Some, even children, drank rubbing alcohol or sniffed glue or paint thinner when they could get it, just to escape the hurt and hopelessness of their lives and to stop the horrors in their minds.

"Market was the happy time, so the most people I saw were there. The restaurants, cars, food and language were all new to me. I was overwhelmed, but I promised myself I would learn everything I could, so I would be able to help my family. When we were given the house to live in, we were so happy but still afraid, too. The priest welcomed us, but he never told us how long we would be there, so every day I wondered if we could stay or need to go somewhere else. I believed I would never be able to go home, but my mother kept talking about going back, and eventually she did go back to visit.

"The first thing that really bothered me was we did not have enough food. It is true we had a good shelter, but I was hungry all the time. The bread and beans were so limited. Hunger clouded every day, but we got used to it. Above everything else, I really missed our tortillas. Clothing was provided by the priest but that was limited, too. The Sisters had a charitable organization that provided some secondhand clothing—just the basics, no shoes—but we were grateful.

"My mother got used to her new surroundings eventually. I kept thinking about how it used to be, remembering my mother whistling as she cooked my favorites on an open fire—tortillas and beans—and of course there would be fresh coffee. Now she cooked, but she often had very little food to give us, and she did not seem as happy. Her stove was made from three rocks that formed a triangle base, and we would find branches from trees in the nearby mountains that kept the fires burning. There was a white tree that burned better than the others. They called it *Encino* in Spanish. There were many, like the maple in Canada, but soon it was all chopped down.

"My oldest sister, Odilia Marina Tecu, was already living in Guatemala City. She was studying under the leadership of the nuns. We had not seen her since the day after the disappearance of our two brothers. Eventually, about six to eight months after we came here, she found out we were staying with the priest and she came to visit. We were so happy to see her. After that she came to visit whenever she could. One day, I noticed a woman walking into the busier part of the city. She was yelling: 'Relleno! Relleno.' Soon people were coming to her to buy this food. We found out *rellenos* are stuffed mashed plantain filled with black beans and then fried. I thought to myself, my sister and I could start another business, too, but I was concerned it would be hard because I did not yet understand Spanish. We had done well selling wood right after we arrived, so I figured this could work. My sister Odilia encouraged us and gave us five *quatzales* ($1.25 American) to start our own business. We bought fresh corn, cooked it and sold it on the streets. We did not have to know much Spanish to get customers. I think they were attracted by the smell.

"After a few months, my sisters and I were sent to an elementary school about ten minutes away by walking from where we were living. I wore a uniform for school and after a year the knees and part of the butt was worn out and I never had underwear, but I still had to wear it. There were many people like this. Poverty was extreme. We didn't usually notice each other but some made fun of us. We could not communicate with each other even though we were suffering the same. We all spoke different languages, more than ten languages, but we were forced to learn in Spanish.

I wanted to be part of the church youth program when I first arrived, but I needed to be 14. That did not stop me, I would just go anyway. The priest kicked me out many times. That was the beginning of my leadership. That is where I started to learn Spanish. Often in school I was punished, beaten with sticks, my ears pulled. I peed my pants several times when they made me stand with hands up for long periods of time in front of my classmates, because I didn't respond when I should. I just did not know the language. Besides my family, there were only three or four more families from our department in Guatemala."

The home where Jeremias and his family lived had a bathroom. Others had only buckets of water for washing themselves. The latrines accommodated hundreds of people. In those communities, human waste was everywhere. Jeremias said that even though the latrines in his community were well maintained, the smell was horrible all the time, a constant reminder of their displacement and status in this new place. Getting used to the many changes kept him on guard. Even what appeared to be a good change could be unsettling. The beds at the new house were from a store, a mattress with springs and a frame. In traditional communities, like the one from which Jeremias and his family had escaped, people preferred to sleep on the floor with palm mats. So, even this change brought less sleep for quite a while, instead of more.

Thousands of people were trying to survive in this new community, so it took only a few months for all the wood in the immediate area to be gone. That is when Jeremias and his 7-year-old sister went into another business. They left at 5 am and went deep into the thick forest to find the wood that could best be used for cooking fires: cedar and pine, and of course more of the white tree when they could find it. Although the pair of them probably weighed less than 100 pounds, they carried it in large bundles on their backs and distributed it to other sojourners in exchange for food or other wares, occasionally earning up to five quetzales a day. That was enough for a meal for a family of five, with some left over. Jeremias was proud to be taking care of his family. By 7:30 in the morning, he was at school until everyone left at 12:30 for lunch. He loved going to school, even though he didn't understand the language. Then it was back to the woods to gather more branches and firewood.

"I felt proud and good about it," says Jeremias. "My mother was happy, and it helped our family. I still kept up my schoolwork and did so well in elementary school I got a scholarship to go to a private school. I was happy but I was still struggling with the feelings inside of me."

This was a hard time for Jeremias. He speaks about it softly: "I was so sad that the local people were making fun of us. If you were out after dark you would be attacked for sure. This was hard for me because I was usually a gentle person, but the rage inside of me was growing. The first time I knocked someone down who called me a name I felt good, but later I cried because that was not really me. I didn't know what was happening to me.

"They would call us 'Indians—*Indio*.' That was the most negative word you could be called. It meant I was a *nobody*. So even today when I hear this it bothers me. After six months, in my first year in middle school, the Sisters from another school for orphans hired me to teach. The school was a 20-minute walk away in the city suburb. I was able to help support my family, so I felt very proud. It helped me not to think about what I had seen, or the bad things still happening.

"From age 12 to 15, I came into contact with children from many other communities and countries, and although our stories were very much the same, the languages and our own mistrust separated us. We had our territories, and there were many bullies and much fighting. I was beaten badly by some of these children when I was 11 and 12 years old.

"I felt the anger growing inside of me. I was not a fighter, but I sometimes wanted to destroy everyone who ever hurt me or any of my family. I felt that rage. I finished high school in 1991 and graduated in October. This was a big accomplishment. Then I started at San Carlos De Guatemala University (USAC) in January 1992, to study to become a middle and high school teacher, with a minor in Psychology. In the meantime, I also started to work full time as a community developer for Casa Alianza."

Casa Alianza is an international non-profit organization and the Latin American branch of Covenant House. It is a charity and NGO, whose aims are the rehabilitation and defense of street children.

"I attended classes, did homework at night, and worked all day," Jeremias explains. "I was with Casa Alianza one year. Then I worked with CONFREGUA (Conferencia de Religiosos de Guatemala) programs, funded by the United Nations Refugee Agency (UNHCR), with refugees to Mexico, and stayed with this organization until I came to Canada. I decided to make that anger I still carried work for me, to push me harder to succeed."

Jeremias has a heart for young people who suffer in silence like he once did. He knows the pain and how hard it is to find relief, or even someone else who can help. Many people look at the behaviours and back away. Well-meaning therapists use canned programs to treat those who have suffered trauma, and often make things worse. Jeremias wanted to change this, and still tries actively today. Jeremias met the girl who was to be his future wife just before he started high school. She caught his eye when he went to visit his sister at the school they both attended. It was a Christian school for girls in grades one to six, tightly run by the nuns.

He tells this story with a smile: "I saw Soledad for the first time when she was 10 or 11 years old. I was almost 13 and I was visiting my sister, Alba. Most of the students were poor or indigenous girls from all of the parts of the country. The first time I saw Soledad she was playing the marimba. I was impressed. She was very little, but she sounded like a professional player. She was so tiny she needed a stair steps to be able to reach that big musical instrument.

"I was very interested in meeting and talking to Soledad, but obviously it couldn't happen because of her age, and because the school was strict. I remember I felt so very sad at the time that I could not get a chance to talk to her. Another time, when

I got to visit my sister, I told her that there's a little girl that I would love to meet and talk to. I was surprised to find out Soledad was my sister's friend, so the next time I visited I got the opportunity to talk to her. That made me happy.

"Since we were both kids, it was no more than friendship, but I looked forward to the times I would see her. I was 14 the last time I saw Soledad for a long time, because I started my middle school in an intern institute for indigenous males. That meant I would be expected to help with teaching other younger students as I progressed in my own education. After almost four years, Soledad switched school and went to the institute for indigenous females in Antigua, Guatemala.

"We were both older now, so when I saw her again, my attraction to her was more serious. When I got a chance to tell her my admiration for her and the crush I had on her, she was surprised and also cried, because she never expected that from me. She was upset and angry at first. My sister was again at the same school as Soledad, so I started to visit more frequently. It was a lot of hassle, because the institute was run by nuns and very strictly, too. However, I was known by the sisters as a really polite young man, so I got the privilege of visiting my sister, and obviously Soledad too. I told Soledad when she was in grade nine that she was the one for me, and that I would like her to be my love and that one day I would marry her. It was not until after graduation from high school that things became more serious."

As soon as Jeremias' family realized he was dating Soledad, they wanted them to marry as soon as possible. In fact, there was considerable pressure from several family members for the couple to get married. Jeremias says he would have been prepared to live with Soledad without the nuptials, but Guatemalan culture frowns heavily on such practices. The families were not happy with any living arrangement that was not formally sanctioned by a marriage ceremony.

5

Father's Unexpected Return

While still in university, Jeremias received a huge shock. He recalls that day:

"We had always assumed my father had been killed by the army, but I was to have the shock of my life. I was in university and out doing a community project with the priest when I saw a man walking toward me. I thought I saw a ghost. I didn't know how to react. I just stood there. 'You've grown a lot,' he said to me in our language. He was crying and trying to explain why he had to go and how the priests had hidden him. I cried but did not talk for a while. I felt much anger and I was not sure why.

"When I finally spoke, I was not as angry. 'It is good to be safe,' I told him, 'but you had a family. You should have told us. It was selfish to make us think you were kidnapped or dead.'

'I had no time, and it was safer for you to not know,' was all he said.

He tried to show no emotion as he came back to where we lived. My mother started to cry. She didn't hug him or show any feelings toward him. She had always talked about how bad their relationship was. I don't know if her tears were from sadness or relief. She gave him some food and they went to talk in private."

Jeremias explains to me that what his father did during his time away was never discussed. Whatever secrets there were would remain concealed. Jeremias had mixed feelings for a very long time. On the one hand, he respected his father for what he had done to help his community and for his wisdom. But he also remembered his excessive drinking, and the fact that his father never once told him he loved him or praised him for any accomplishment. Jeremias tells me he cannot remember a time when his father played with him as a child, or really spent any time with him at all. As he continues his story, he points out that he is thankful he came to be close to his father in the past few years just before coming to Canada, and he learned to forgive any mistakes of the past.

"After that, my father was very gentle with us, but I don't think my mother was happy to have him home. He had been gone more than ten years. She took care of him, but that was all, I think. He started to work with the church again, and later, as a social worker, with a non-governmental organization (NGO) funded by the priest. We did not talk about his time away from us."

After Jeremias started university, just two months after graduation from high school, he continued to work. He would work 8 am until 4 pm and attend university from 6 pm until 10 pm. On the weekends he attended classes from 9am until 12 pm, and often worked the rest of the day. But not everyone was as faithful to the cause, and it soon became time to move to a new level to help his people.

Jeremias graduated from university in 1994. He taught at the middle school and high school levels and he loved it. He was a teacher like his father, and he felt proud of this. He still had unresolved feelings about his father's disappearance, but he was happy he could honour him in this way. He knew how much his father valued education, so now as a teacher he was keeping these traditions and beliefs alive. Jeremias was also a hard worker like his father. His first formal full-time job was immediately after high school in 1991. There was an NGO, the Ecumenical Guatemalan Hope and Fraternity Foundation, which provided development programs for immigrants from other parts of Guatemala. He worked with youth. With the help of the priest who funded this organization, youth programs were started for children.

"We wanted to deal with violence," he says. "Different groups were forming gangs and they were establishing territories. It was growing worse. We got together to clean up the community, to help them have a sense of pride and to feel better about where they were living. We helped, too, because we could teach by doing. Then we would play soccer."

For Jeremias, putting it all together just seemed to come naturally. He explains: "I was good at writing proposals, so I was successful in getting money to help with the specific needs of youth and getting a school, or maybe having things like coffee and bread in a place where food was scarce. After two or three years, we were able to erect a building to hold special events like dances and gatherings. We still played soccer. It was a favorite for all of us. We even held an election for queen and king of the community. Teachers and other people were judges. We knew it promoted self-esteem and solidarity. Children did not talk about the horrors behind them. There was still so much fear and distrust preventing anyone from talking about anything. Things sometimes opened up when we were playing soccer. The first time a kid came to me and told me what happened to his father, I realized I was not alone in my experiences."

Jeremias was required to go to other communities. In the field it was often quite dirty. He took three different buses to get there, more than an hour. He would wake up early and take the first bus at 5:45 am and the last one home at 7:30 pm. He hoped to organize community representatives, so they could resolve problems such as contaminated drinking water, bridges that had been destroyed, lack of health services and of food. He worked in Zone 18 with four communities: El Llano, El Sapote, Llano Largo and El Chato. His office was in a cement block building with a metal roof, but he spent most of his days outside talking to people.

"Most of this job was community networking," he explains. "I had office hours, and I wrote reports. I really liked the job because I was connecting with people, and I wanted to help them. I was there 10 -12 months. Sometimes I even worked on weekends."

He clarifies: "After one year I left that organization. I resigned. Not everyone there was dedicated to working hard for the people.

A month later, I was approached by a priest who knew me. He said he was impressed by the work I had been doing in the communities. He was impressed by my young age and what he had seen me overcome. He wanted someone honest to apply for a job with *Conferencia de Religiosos de Guatemala (CONFREGUA)*, where he was treasurer. He said the job would be with the Office of Multiple Services. Since they dealt with refugees and communities that had been affected by the war, and because of the volatile political climate still there, there was caution around the stating of the actual mandate. He invited me to apply and I did."

For Jeremias, this decision carried fear. He explains: "I was so nervous. I didn't know if I could do it. Part of the job would be to negotiate between guerillas and the government and to oversee the returns and provide lands for the returning refugees from Mexico. I liked working in the field but dealing with politicians scared me, and it was not something I really wanted to do. Still, I saw how it could help."

Jeremias met this priest on a weekend when he was visiting his family. He had been joking about wanting a job, but the priest was serious. The following Monday, Jeremias met with Sister Maria Nieves from Spain, the director of the programs.

He describes this important turning point: "I was very shy and nervous. She took my face with her two hands and said, 'Welcome.' I was surprised. I told her what I had been doing and she was so nice. I told her some of my story, and she said she couldn't believe everything that had happened to me. We talked for a while, but she didn't tell me anything about the job.

She just said, 'Welcome Aboard' and showed me the office. I didn't know what was happening. She showed me a computer and books and talked about how much they could pay me. She told me they really needed someone they could trust. They said they had to fire others in the past because this is important work, and confidentiality and diplomacy were most important.

"I told her I didn't know if I could do it. For one thing, I could not use a computer and didn't have a car. I was overwhelmed. The trust they were putting in me seemed too big. I thanked her and asked her to give me time to learn. She just smiled and said: 'Get out of my office and come back tomorrow and work.'"

Jeremias went home and told his family. His mother assured him he could do it. And soon he found that out for himself. After only three weeks, he was driving the Toyota Land Cruiser they gave him. He was determined to make his mother proud, to live up to her expectations of him. He was the new Director of Programs.

"I had only been working about a month when I had to go to my first official meeting," he says. "Only two of us were from my organization, and we went to meet an official from the UNHCR refugee organization and representative of the office of Guatemala. They call this a mission of the United Nations in Guatemala. There were representatives from the different refugee camps in Mexico, where there were hundreds of refugee camps. There they could get citizenship, but if they wanted to return to Guatemala—and 80% wanted to—these negotiations needed to ensure that human rights were observed. On the national level, we asked for land and security and to abort any type of military missions close to these communities. We were also there to represent the people at the community group level.

"The first time I attended one of these meetings I was shocked. I did not feel prepared. It was too much for my heart. I felt anger rising up. It resurrected something inside me I thought was buried. I had lots of feelings, but I did not speak that first time. The second time I did speak, and I was prepared."

At this point, Jeremias was still in university, but he had an understanding supervisor. She allowed him to work out a schedule after negotiating with the professors. Still, it was a heavy schedule—seven days a week—even for a strong young man in his early twenties. And, also at this point Jeremias was not yet married and wanted to spend time with Soledad. It was a tough balancing act, and often his desire to help his people won his time.

"Sometimes on weekends I would see my girlfriend," he says. "It was so busy we didn't get much time together. She worked in Guatemala City at a school for special needs students. I had almost given up on our relationship. Sometimes I even felt annoyed when I got a phone call in the middle of my studies or my job. I was too devoted to my work. That is probably what made me decide to get married. We had talked about living together so we could see each other more, but my dad was very angry when he heard this. That left us only one thing to do—to get married. We got married after a lot pressure from both our parents and other relatives. Culturally speaking, families and relatives have the right to push, and they all agreed we had an obligation to get married, because they did not want us to prostitute ourselves or our families. It threatened the prestige of the family and our cultural values. We gave in even though we might not have been ready for it."

Jeremias and Soledad were married on January 28, 1993, in Lo de Fuentes, Mixco, Guatemala, attended by many relatives and friends from Guatemala as well as many international friends from Jeremias' work, including some from Canada. Close to 500 people attended the celebration. Some stayed for one or both ceremonies. Others came only to the party afterwards. The party lasted more than 24 hours to accommodate both Catholic and traditional Mayan ceremonies. Marimbas shared the dance floor with more modern disco tunes.

The Mayan ceremony was led by Jeremias' father, assisted by the Catholic priest who later heard their vows in a Christian ceremony. As a Mayan priest, the elder Tecu opened the ceremony beside the sacred fire, where everyone was invited to make an offering to bless the couple. Candles, flowers, *pom* (a kind of incense), even bread, sugar and cinnamon were thrown into the fire before the Mayan priest prayed to the four directions, reminiscent of indigenous ceremonies the world over, and performed an ancient dance to bring happiness and blessings to Jeremias and Soledad. Then everyone who had been invited for this special ceremony came to offer words of blessing and encouragement to the couple in person.

Jeremias and Soledad wore traditional Achi dress for the occasion, and their heads were covered—hers with a bright white cloth called a *velo* and his with a brightly colored cloth adorned with symbols and pictures of animals called a *tzute*. This is a Mayan term generally used for a cloth used for ceremonial purposes and woven on a back-strap loom. There were no rings to exchange, but the couple was encircled by a necklace of flowers, which they held together during the ceremony, then offered to the fire at the end. Before moving on to the Catholic ceremony, which was attended by even more people, the couple thanked everyone for their help.

At the Catholic Church, Soledad was attended by her mother, grandmother, and brother. Jeremias' father, mother and sisters stood with him. The church was full. There were guests from Canada, England, Poland, and the United States—all people who had worked with Jeremias. Since the marriage was really a community event, Jeremias' sisters had assistance making food for the party. Hundreds of tamales were prepared in the two days before the wedding. There was a great deal of alcohol and music also. The band played for 10 hours with only a few breaks. When they could play no more, the CDs took over for many more hours. Jeremias and his new bride celebrated with their friends, taking short naps in one of the family homes from time to time. It was a celebration not soon forgotten, but not without some conflict. Jeremias tells of an unexpected confrontation with his father.

"It was about two in the morning," he says. "I needed some more money to pay the band so they would keep playing. I asked my father, but he was very drunk. He punched me in the chest and told me the party was over. I was shocked, since he was the one who pushed the hardest for us to get married, but I could see there was no reasoning with him when he was so drunk. We argued, but eventually things calmed down. He handed me the money to give to the band and we just went back to partying. Still, it was something I found hard to forget."

At the time of the wedding, Jeremias was working at Alianza Para El Desarollo Comunitario, an organization devoted to the planning and implementation of programs intended to promote community development, and raise the standard of living for people displaced from their homes. Soledad was still employed at a home for people with special needs (Casa Nazaret). Both were also enrolled in a local university. It would be Soledad's first year. She planned to be a lawyer.

Jeremias had been given two weeks of vacation and Soledad had not yet started her course work, so the couple could enjoy some rare uninterrupted time together. They spent the first few days after the party resting and visiting with family. It took a week to open all the gifts. They had everything they needed for their future home. The second week, the couple went to visit Soledad's mother for a few days, before going off on their own to enjoy the scenery in Panajachel, a town in the southwestern Guatemalan Highlands, less than 90 miles from Guatemala City, in the department of Solola. For three days, the newlyweds enjoyed the majesty of Lake Atitlán, the deepest lake in Central America, which is one of the country's main tourist attractions even today. Before the marriage, Jeremias' father had given him a piece of land. Now it was time to build a house close to his family, for this new Tecu family and those yet to come.

6

Balancing Family and Work

When Jeremias learned he was to become a father for the first time, he was overcome with emotions.

"We were riding home on a bus together when Soledad told me she might be pregnant. I was surprised but very happy. I always wanted to be a dad. I was joking around with my wife, but she was worried. Later I went with my wife so she could have the test and it was positive. My wife cried. I think she was nervous and did not feel prepared. I told her it would be okay, not to cry because the baby might feel rejected. But I cried also. I was filled with so many emotions. I wanted to run and tell all my friends and all the people about the good news. I always dreamed about being a father. It is such a gift. I felt so blessed, so happy.

"Our first baby was born in Guatemala City. We decided to pay a midwife to attend Soledad, but when I brought Soledad to first meet the lady, she invited me to be there also and to help during the birth. I was weak just thinking about it. I told her, 'Oh my God, no, in this condition I'm not really good at helping. I do not want to see my wife cry or be in pain'. Even though I had seen much suffering in my life, I just knew I could not watch this even for a minute, so I told her to call me after the baby arrived and I would come as soon as possible.

"Soledad's pregnancy went well. She continued to work and go to university until a few days before the baby was born. She was very active. I was still working, traveling a lot, sometimes to Mexico, and I only got home two or three times per week, sometimes only once a week or less. The night Soledad went into labour, I was at home. When she started, I called the midwife and we went to her house, about 20 minutes away by car. She offered a bed for me to stay, so maybe I could help. I knew I could not stay. I did not sleep much that night. I was crying and praying to God to please help make everything okay. When the midwife called me around nine am, I was so nervous. When I heard her tell me 'Congratulations, Dad; you have a healthy baby boy,' I was overcome with the joy of that moment. I felt so grateful. I remember I kneeled and thanked God for such a blessing. Then I ran crying to tell my mom who lived next door and asking her to please come with me.

"We went to shop for my baby boy. We bought some clothing and diapers. I was so excited. When I first saw my son, I was so overcome with happiness, but I was afraid to hold him. My mom held him. I thought his face was so ugly, all squished up and a funny color. I asked my mom if that was how he should look, and she laughed. Soledad and the baby came back with us. My family was so excited. At the time, I did not think he resembled any of us. I decided his name would be Oscar Juan Pablo. Soledad wanted to name him after me, but I did not like the idea. Instead I chose Oscar, in memory of my brother Oscar. Juan was in memory of my grandpa and also my first name is Juan. And Pablo was in memory of one the most memorable male leaders in Baja Verapaz, my great grandpa.

"The first time I held Oscar, I was nervous. He was delicate. I was afraid I would break his leg or arm by holding him. I felt proud. Things changed a lot with the new baby. Neither of us got much sleep, especially my wife. We were busy all the time. She went back to work after a month and returned to school within two weeks. Sometimes she took Oscar to university so she could feed him. Sometimes I could help. Other times, a friend might help while she wrote her exams. It was a lot with a new baby and doing our post-secondary education, plus full-time work. At night, we were taking turns to sleep. With the baby, it was really hard. Soledad sometimes cried, because at times the baby was crying a lot and we did not know what to do. She was exhausted and concerned there might be something wrong, but my mother came and gave us a hand, and explained that it is normal for babies to sometimes cry a lot. Somehow, we got through it and came to love our little son more every day. Life seemed better, and there were times I could forget the horrors of the past, especially when I held my son. I thought maybe now things were sure to get better. We had no idea what was yet to come."

It was part of Jeremias' job to go to the camps in Mexico, but he did not feel ready right away, so he did some research first. He decided to talk to someone who had been there before. He heard about a priest, Father Ricardo Falla. He had read one of his books about his experiences in the jungle villages, where the military had persecuted civilians and they had escaped to the jungle. They had been accused of being guerillas. The priest described in his book how he had entered through Mexico to get to these villages. He saw bodies everywhere and definite signs of great torture.

One community was Ixcan. Most people did not even know these communities existed. Eventually the Father had to go to Spain for safety. Jeremias spoke to a priest who knew him, because he had read about how they had to escape to Mexico. He wanted to know their background before he worked with them. When the time came, he approached them humbly and wore his traditional clothes. He spoke Mayan to anyone who could understand, as a sign of respect. This trip had a great impact on Jeremias.

He recalls: "It was the children who affected me so much. I worked with adults, but I played soccer with the children after I ate. I remembered what it was like to play soccer with no shoes. We had used a makeshift soccer ball made with leaves and plastic bags. Here we had real soccer balls. The children didn't talk much, but I know they looked forward to those soccer games. I saw the hunger in the face of the children, with sad eyes too used to being overlooked. But I was so busy meeting with officials I didn't have the time I wanted to spend with them.

"What bothered me the most when I looked around at the camps was the starvation, and people sitting around with no purpose in their lives. It bothered me a lot. Poverty in Guatemala usually meant you had very little, but at least you had something to eat, and you worked to help each other. In the refugee camps, it is worse than poverty. There is not enough of anything and little hope. It made me sad to hear the stories. I had no answers to give to the many questions, mainly 'Why?' I often felt angry inside and I used that to keep working. I still do. I had a good boss and that helped. Many times at night I couldn't sleep. We had a tent and a sleeping bag. I wasn't afraid. It was the sadness and the anger. It wrapped around me like a blanket.

"Would they ever get back to Guatemala? I wondered. I knew this was not really living. Many ate from garbage cans. Just being alive is precious, but just being alive is not enough; people need some place where they belong, something that is theirs, like a home. When you are a refugee you really have no home. I wanted everyone to have a home. I said this in our meetings; we need to give them land. It was theirs in the beginning. All who supported the peace agreement agreed."

For Jeremias, the memories of his own experiences made him all the more committed to be there. He didn't live by a watch. He just worked until he could do no more. He worked to make a difference, and only occasionally stopped to rest for a while or eat. He carried three phones and could expect a call about an emergency at any time, so there was no way to make it a nine-to-five job.

He describes one of these times: "We were visiting Pueblo Nuevo and supervising a housing project. At night we slept in a storage shed with no lights. It was a jungle. There was still civil war. Once they came with flashlights in the middle of the night. The military base was only minutes away and usually to see light at night meant the military were going to fight. Strangely, I was feeling afraid that night even before the lights came. I was expecting the worst, so I told my colleagues: 'Anything that is going to happen right now, I want you to know I love you all. Don't be afraid; just tell the truth.'

"We were prepared and braced for an unpleasant encounter, but when the door opened, it was not the military. It was two brothers, and one of their wives was about to have a baby. I do not like blood, so I wanted no part in delivering a baby. It was a three-hour drive to a nurse, so I was the driver. The woman was crying harder and harder as we drove. I was sweating and trying to concentrate on driving. My colleague was nervous also. I stopped after almost two hours near a place with water. I asked her husband if he knew what to do. She had the baby there. I helped deliver, not knowing at all what I was doing. After cleaning the baby up and wrapping him in my jacket we headed to the clinic another hour and a half away. I was in shock. My colleague was shaking when I asked what to do. My mother had told me years before how she measured the cord with her fingers, to know where to cut it and tie it off. I don't even know how I remembered that. I cried. The husband cried. The baby cried and then the adults began to laugh."

Jeremias continued to study for his degree. It was hard with a child and the job. In 1996, he finally graduated. He still only saw his family on the weekends, sometimes only once or twice a month. Oscar was a baby, but before he even realized it Jeremias returned from work to see he was walking. He'd missed watching him grow. He admits he was more married to his job than to his family.

"I personalized the job I had," he admits. "It consumed me and was more important than anything. Was I trying to heal my own wounds or help others? I still do not know. My wife was very patient in the beginning. We talked about how important the work was. We didn't talk about what it was like to be alone most of the time with a baby. I trusted her to do a good job. I knew she could do a good job as both the mom and dad, just like my mom had to do for so many years. I never made the connection in my mind that I could be expecting too much of my wife."

Things stayed that way for the next few years. Even when his wife became pregnant for the second time, Jeremias was still away working most of the time. Oscar was almost three years old when Jeremias found out his wife was pregnant with their second child. To be sure, they booked a visit to a private clinic so she could have a pregnancy test. Jeremias was excited but his wife, tired from caring for their home and baby most of the time by herself, was not as enthusiastic. It was some time before Jeremias realized just how hard his absences were on her.

"When my wife told me that maybe she was pregnant she was a bit sad and confused," he says. "When we got the result, which was positive, I was so happy I never thought about what she might be feeling. I told her this news deserved a celebration and I took her to a cafeteria so we could eat and celebrate our second baby news."

This was a hard time for Soledad. With a toddler and the demands of a home and pregnancy, she was often worn out. Still, she managed to keep everything together, and looked forward to the times when her husband would be home.

"When I came home, I would take my son for a ride and buy him an ice cream and special treats," Jeremias says. "We were so happy, and my wife always seemed happy to see me, too."

However, Soledad was getting very depressed, and Jeremias did not recognize this. The doctor was the first one to point it out. She wasn't eating. She became thin despite her pregnancy, and still Jeremias missed the signs. He was consumed by his work. He realizes now that his wife was probably burying her anger, and only let it out many years later in Canada. Work was still his first priority. He continued in the refugee camps, and things changed in 1998 that made the situations even more intense. Demands were now being made by the organization to the courts to get permission to conduct exhumations. It was a fight that lasted two years and Jeremias was engaged in the process.

It was around this time that he found a new way to alleviate some of his stress: he started drinking. He was a hard worker, and sometimes his colleagues would go for a drink after work. He had seen his father drink too much. He also knew one of the things his wife liked the most about him when they met was that he did not drink or smoke, so he had always refused. But now he felt overwhelmed. The frustration of his work and the wounds from his past were creating an emotional anguish that just would not go away. So, when a colleague asked him one day to go for a beer he went, not even sure if he would actually drink. His friend talked about how hard it was to deal with hearing all the stories. He pointed out that children as young as ten in his culture drank to forget their problems. That is when Jeremias decided he wanted freedom from the pain too. Using alcohol to self-medicate would be another battle he would fight for many years to come.

"One day I was really mad because of the frustration of trying to help people and watching them lose hope," he explains. "When others refused to believe the stories of genocide, it frustrated me. I drank that day, several, one after the other. Soon it became a tradition from Thursday to Sunday to drink, a tradition that I came to regret, something I struggled with for a long time."

The second baby was born in the (IGSS) Instituto Guatemalteco de Seguridad Social, a public government hospital open to anyone who pays taxes. In many ways it resembled a private hospital, but it did not allow fathers to be close to their wives during the birthing process. So, Jeremias continued to work even when Soledad's due date came closer. In fact, at the minute his new daughter was born he was traveling from his workplace. He had already made arrangements before leaving Guatemala City with his brother-in-law to make sure his wife got to the hospital, and his son Oscar to a babysitter. Unfortunately, the ride was delayed, which turned out to make things harder for his wife.

He relates: "When my second child was born, I was still working for CONFREGUA. It was so difficult for me to be with my family as a normal dad. I felt very much in love with my work, but I also loved my son and wife. I had to travel most of the time. I just spent a couple of days each week with my family. I always believed and trusted my wife that everything was okay, and that she would be taking good care of our son and unborn baby. I really enjoyed spending time with them when I was around. I played with my son and cooked for all of us. But I realize today my wife suffered a lot from having so much responsibility while I was gone so much. I think sometimes she thought I cared more about my work than my family. I don't think she or my new baby daughter ever forgave me for being away for this birth.

"Our second child was named Mayte Mercedes—*May* because when a woman is pregnant, this is the *baby place inside mom* in Maya Achi language. *Te* is *mother* in another Mayan language. Mercedes, my grandmother's name on my mother's side, was in honour of her sacrifice and contribution to the community. She was a healer and a midwife, a very brilliant woman. For me, my children's names represented our success and history, memories that no one wrote down, so through my children I believed we could celebrate and keep their legacy. We hired a babysitter to help us with the babies. Oscar was growing, and since he was the first grandchild in the Tecu family he was often with a family member and went from house to house. My family loved him very much. Having a second baby added some stress for us, but not in comparison to learning how to care for our first child.

"I felt so happy I was working at something that was really meaningful for me, and that I had a family like I always dreamed about. I was so thankful! I had everything. Being around my son, Oscar, was really emotional, and with my new baby I felt like the happiest man and father in the entire world. At home, since all the Tecu family lived in the same community, it was so busy. My wife was doing her law studies. I was working full time, plus completing my post-secondary studies. When I got back from my work travels, I usually cooked and invited all my relatives and our neighbours and friends. It was a happy time for me, but I know it was much harder for my wife who took care of the home every day.

"I have the privilege to be the oldest son, so my children were the first grandchildren for my parents. They really enjoyed my children, and my mother spent a lot of time with them, since she was home most of the time. My father was working, but in his free times he would hug and play with my babies. Both of them gave my children a lot of important teachings about Mayan cultural values and customs."

The pull between work and home life was a real struggle for Jeremias and put a strain on the marriage. He realizes today his wife did not understand his passionate commitment to help others. Sometimes he did not understand it himself, but he was driven to make a difference for the people still suffering in his country.

He explains: "The hardest thing, I guess, was how to combine work and family. I was so disappointed because I loved my job and wanted to put all my effort there, but I still wanted to be with my children and enjoy them. I guess my work won that battle. I felt I had to concentrate on it. At the time, the Guatemalan political situation was turning very violent, and it wasn't even safe for me and my colleagues because of our work in the Mexican refugee camps. We were helping the returnees and advocating for human rights. That meant we would bring genocide cases to court, and work on the recompilation of histories and exhumation of clandestine cemeteries.

"I didn't really like this part of my life because of the risks that I had to take, but I knew how important it was. I felt like I had no choice. This was what I was meant to do. The work sometimes was my life and my survival, but I worried about the dangers, especially because indirectly my family was involved, too, and might not be safe."

7

Connecting with Breaking the Silence

Jeremias continued to work in the refugee camps in Mexico for eight years until 1999. His main job was to help refugees resettle in Guatemala, but he also did advocacy work and collected stories from other survivors so they could be used in court. It was important to him to collect the history so the children would never forget what happened. This was almost an impossible task because everyone in Guatemala was fearful. The unspoken code was: *If someone in your family was killed, keep quiet so you won't have it happen to you.*

In addition to paid employment, Jeremias volunteered with many organizations, with support from his boss, so he could get funding through proposals. The New Hope Foundation was a priority for him. He was very committed to opening up opportunities for children to be educated. He also supported other movements focused on aiding the people of Guatemala to protect their basic human rights—movements like CODECA (Comité de Desarrollo Campesino) and the Farmer's Committee of the Highlands (Comité Campesino del Altiplano: CCDA)—that promoted the development of farming and indigenous communities in Guatemala to increase their standard of living, so the people would be able to gain income from working in a co-op.

In Eastern Canada, at this time, a network of people concerned about injustices in Guatemala was being formed. It was to become an important part of Jeremias' future. Breaking the Silence (BTS) was, and still remains, a voluntary network of people in the Maritimes who began to organize in 1988 to support the efforts of Guatemalans struggling for political, social, and economic justice. As a community of people who share this commitment to solidarity, they still undertake advocacy and lobbying; organize delegations; send interns, volunteers, and human rights accompaniers; promote fair-trade coffee, and raise awareness within their own communities through speaking tours by Guatemalan leaders and other political campaigns. The interns and volunteers regularly travel to Guatemala to work with local villages. For many years, there has been a campaign of support for Guatemalan communities resisting actions by Canadian mining companies. They also train and send Canadians to act as international observers and witnesses to human rights violations and threats. Today, Jeremias remains part of this organization in Canada and still sells BTS Fair Trade coffee that comes from the community where he once worked, San Lucas Toliman. He says he owes them so much gratitude. In fact, it was the accompaniment by BTS that eventually led to the safe escape of Jeremias and his family from Guatemala to Canada. He met several BTS people while working in Mexico.

Jeremias believed firmly that the silence needed to be broken in order for people and the land to heal. He knew it was important for the people to talk among themselves and with others so they could help each other. BTS could help this happen.

"We needed to share our pain and anger and have a chance to question WHY," he points out. But work continued to control his life.

"I put a lot of energy here," he says. "I continued to channel the deep anger inside me this way, but I felt too attached to it. It consumed me. I soon learned that many had lost their relatives, who had been discarded in a common clandestine cemetery. When I heard about that, I said we had to do something."

8

Exhumations

Jeremias' first experience with exhumation was with Comité de Desarrollo Campesino (CODECA) at Santo Domingo Suchitepeques. Since 1992, this organization has been working on improving the situation of the rural poor in Guatemala, focusing on issues such as the wage conditions for farmers, land reform and nationalization of electric energy in the country. Jeremias started to work more with the people, the farmers who grew their corn and beans, the poor people, both indigenous and not, the *campesinos*. His main work was still considered to be as a negotiator with the government and guerrillas, but as he felt more connected to the actual people, he knew he had to help in new ways. That eventually meant helping them get exhumations to find their lost loved ones.

He was approached by a small group to do this. At that time in Guatemala there was still a great deal of violence and insecurity. It was a risk to talk to members of any organization or community. No one knew for sure who could be trusted. As Jeremias explains, it took a great deal of courage for the people to approach him, and even more courage for Jeremias to respond as he did.

"One of the community representatives introduced himself as an active member of the URNG (Guatemalan National Revolutionary

Unity)," he explains. "The organization that I was working for was really strict with their policies. We were not supposed to help or support any groups that were related to any political point of view. But when I heard their stories and listened very sincerely to their concerns and what they wanted, it touched me deep inside because we had pretty similar stories. As our conversation went on, I discovered this group of people was not representing any organization. Their concerns and sadness were with their murdered and missing loved ones. They wanted peace. They wanted to find their loved ones, and this would mean the exhumation of a common clandestine cemetery, because of a massacre in the 1980s committed by the military. I was told most of the victims were relatives and community members of Santo Domingo Suchitepéquez and neighboring communities.

"I knew it was really hard to get permission to do an exhumation. The politics involved had to be considered. Since the majority of the massacres were committed by the national military, it was obvious that if we were to bring our complaint to any judge, we would have to go through a lot of protocol and we would also be taking personal risks. But despite all the risks and all the process that we knew was there, I saw a community who strongly believed in their struggle. All they were looking for was peace of mind, and maybe some justice for their loved ones.

"Three men and two women came to my office and asked for my help. In the beginning, they hesitated and started to talk about their organization, how they needed to get back their land and human rights, but they didn't explain at first what they meant by this. I asked what they meant by human rights. The leader said, 'We are worried to share with you because we do not trust, but we need some help. I asked permission from my colleagues to share with you.' I told them not to worry, that I would help, and no one would ever know who approached me.

They all started to talk at once; I could see they were relieved. They called me their brother and explained they had been working more than five years with the community, collecting names of all the people who disappeared in war. One of the men said he was kidnapped but escaped. He now believed the way to honour the memories of the mothers, fathers, brothers and sisters, and the ones who did not escape alive, would be to have an exhumation. He said it might now even be for court purposes, but it would give some peace and unite the community because the community was destroyed by the war.

"He said we needed to come together again because many did not trust; they were afraid. Others did not believe it could happen to them, but some shared their stories. He told me they wanted to honour their mom or dad, their relatives who had died, and said they knew where they were buried. Even though it was illegal to go there, they said they needed to offer candles and flowers so their relatives could be happy. They told me they did not deserve to be there alone without their families."

Listening to these pleas, Jeremias was deeply moved and wanted to do something to help. He knew how they felt, he believed what they were saying, and he knew what had to be done. But he was not sure how to proceed.

"When they left, I felt so sad I didn't know what to do," he remembers. "I cried because I connected myself with them. I knew my own brothers might be in one of these graves. I thought to myself, one thing I have is the power to approach places to get money for projects. I decided to tell my boss that this has to happen for justice and for peace for the community, as well as the individuals. I knew how important this was. Culturally speaking, we don't believe our relatives just pass away. We talk to our dead ancestors every day. We visit their graves. These relatives had no graves to visit and no way to have peace. This community felt disconnected. I knew what that felt like. My boss said this was not the first story she had heard like this. She had also wondered how to approach it, and she was happy I talked to her. She said she would write proposals to one of our funders for money to help, and we would support them from beginning to end."

In most communities in Guatemala, the market is an important place for people to gather. To go to the market is a happy event for everyone. People often attended church, and then went shopping and connected with friends. In Rabinal, the market was active on Thursdays, Saturdays, and Sundays. This was the same in most communities. In the days of the massacre, there was one main street that connected the villages, and the military had their base set up so everyone would have to pass by them on their way to the market.

Jeremias heard from one of the people asking for help how one Sunday, coming from market and church, he had witnessed the military raping and torturing people. He said he had also been beaten and thrown into a pit with the remains of other dead people. He was unconscious but survived. When he came to the next morning he escaped. He said he remembered approximately 45 men, women and children had been beaten, raped, tortured, and some burned. He said the fortunate ones were shot. This man witnessed people screaming, and he saw three or four cistern wells filled with bodies. He remembered and said he could identify the place. He cried as he told Jeremias how sometimes 50-100 soldiers would all do this together, and it was all legal.

For Jeremias, these stories cut deep into his heart. Even to recount them was painful.

"I felt so connected with those people. I told them the next time I would come to their community to meet them. I promised to help, and I saw some happiness in their eyes. It was all they had left. Two weeks later I took two team members to visit them, seven hours drive away. We talked with many people and I saw hope. They said we were the first people who really listened to them and wanted to do something. There were many stories. Someone asked me if I wanted to visit the base where this happened. He told me there were no more soldiers there. They had already been moved to a central base.

"Those in power continued to be part of the military, even today, but the regular soldiers were also community people forced to be soldiers. These soldiers were then forced to kill their own people or face torture. They would get away from the military as soon as they could. They had no idea what was going on. They were led to believe they had to defeat the Guerillas because they were all bad, but the Guerillas were fighting to save their country. It was brainwashing—the worst way of doing things. Sometimes it started with good motives that led to the wrong outcomes. Sometimes the Guerilla's power was misused too, but only by a few. The bad ones, they also raped and killed."

The Guatemalan Truth Commission Report, discussed in the book *Memory of Silence*, edited by Daniel Rothenberg (2012), talks about the importance of the exhumation of mass graves and clandestine cemeteries in Guatemala in supporting psychosocial healing and providing closure for the victims and their families. The report said that more than 5,000 bodies were recovered during this process. In Victoria Sanford's *Buried Secrets: Truth and Human Rights in Guatemala*, she details the challenges surrounding the performance of exhumations and includes personal accounts of survivors greatly affected by them. She recognized the exhumations were not only carried out to secure "evidence gathered by forensic archaeologists and forensic anthropologists, but also as the process of the excavation of memory and retaking of public space" for the survivors and those who had been executed.

Sanford worked on the exhumation sites in Rabinal, first in Chichupac and later in Rio Negro. The process to be able to have an exhumation at any site was a lengthy one. First a complaint had to be filed at the Superior Court, and this was usually undertaken by human rights groups. This complaint then had to be approved by the Appeals Court, so it could be sent to the Court of the *Primera Instancia*, the departmental administrative court. If it passed there, the local justice of the peace would be ordered to secure forensic experts who could carry out the exhumation.

In Rabinal, the official forensic doctor only worked part time, and really had no formal training in forensics, so the Guatemalan Forensic Anthropology Foundation (FAFG), for whom Sanford worked, was appointed as the court's expert. She says the Rabinal exhumations were also unique in that they were actually initiated by local residents and not by a human rights group.

Not everyone supported the exhumations. In the beginning, at Rabinal, not even the priests were supportive. Some pastors and politicians likened the exhumations to the work of the anti-Christ and tried to scare the people away. But even stronger was the desire of the people for closure, and a proper funeral for those they had lost. Family members traveled great distances hoping for some evidence of their loved ones—bone fragment, a piece of clothing, shoes or hair that might identify them. Often, when some piece was not identified with an individual, someone would claim it as proof of their family member's remains. Sanford also collected 'more than 400 lengthy testimonies from massacre survivors, former soldiers, civil patrollers, and insurgent combatants in rural areas' during her fieldwork in Guatemala. She says there is no doubt the genocide occurred. The bones do not lie, and the stories are very real.

Jeremias says his work at exhumation sites was very disturbing for him. On one hand, he wanted to bring peace and closure to the many survivors who looked for their loved ones. On the other hand, it brought back to him the horror of the massacre and renewed his longing to find his own two brothers who might very well be in one of these sites.

"I cried a lot during this time," he says. "It's not something I can talk about too much."

For Jeremias, one of the discoveries he still cannot get out of his mind is that of the skeleton of a woman who must have been almost ready to have her baby at the time she was killed. The skeleton of the tiny baby was still there fully formed as part of her, under what was left of her clothing.

9

Danger at Every Turn

Jeremias still enjoyed his work with CONFREGUA. He had been there approximately seven years, and his main focus was resettlement of the returnees from the refugee camps in Mexico. He provided accompaniment and was a witness to make sure that all the commitments given by the national government were honoured. He also helped plan and manage projects such as suitable housing or agriculture that would make life better for the returnees to Guatemala. Overall, this work did not put Jeremias in great jeopardy. The danger for him came from his activism. His voice in striving for basic human rights and justice for his people was getting stronger.

Jeremias explains how he became a target and why: "I was a target because of how our system works. Our country was still militarized even if we had a civil president. The reality is that the one who governs is the military. Obviously, if someone is going to have the courage to talk or speak out against those who committed all the atrocities against our people and our communities, they will jeopardize their life. Genocide was always covered up by the impunity it was given by the dark political machine that was supported by the USA. This is a huge and specialized killing machine—our state machine—with individuals and organizations that were afraid that one day we will uncover the truth to the world and bring them to justice."

Jeremias' workplace had been vandalized several times and the main office broken into on many occasions. Doors and locks were forced open and important documents, disks, computers, and software were taken. Those who worked there also noticed cars following them when they traveled to their work, and often saw suspicious individuals parking in front of or across from the main office. Everyone was on edge. Jeremias suspected he was being stalked and so did his supervisor, who suggested he take some time off and keep a low profile. He tried, but he was not able to keep silent. He felt he needed to keep going. Like others in his office, he felt upset about the break-ins, but he did not anticipate what was to come.

It was May 20, 1999, and Jeremias was on his way to work, like so many days before. He had had a restless night, but he still looked forward to the day. He would be traveling to meet with some of the refugees. But this day was to be different: this day he would be forced to face one of his greatest fears.

Jeremias takes a deep breath as he begins this story: "I was happy and ready to travel as always to help three communities in Las Verapaces, and I left home around 9:30 am. I reached my office around 10 am. I just remember I saw three men walking around the truck that I had just parked as I headed to my workplace. I felt uneasy. As I continued walking to my building, I heard one of them say: '*He is the one*' and suddenly, the last thing I remember is when I tried to turn around, I felt something hit me on the back of my head. I fell down and two men took me and dropped me on the backseat of the truck that I'd just parked. They took my keys and drove away very fast. I did not have any idea what was happening. I couldn't speak. I was partly unconscious, I guess.

"After a period of time, I could hear them speaking and one of them was talking on his cell and said: '*We have him; what is next?*' I felt like I was in a dream, not really awake, but after around 15 minutes I woke up completely. As soon as I woke up, the man who was with me on the back seat pulled his weapon and put it in my mouth, and said that if I moved he was just going to shoot me.

"They started to talk to me by saying that they know everything about me, about my work, about my family, and if I was not going to stop the things that I was involved in something was going to happen to me and my family. Then I heard the other man talking again. He was very upset with his superior, I think, because he just wanted to get rid of me, but somehow their boss was not allowing them to kill me yet. In the meantime, the one who was in charge of me started kicking me in the head. He burned me with his cigarette, and he kept pointing at me with his gun. From the start, after I recovered from the blows to my head, I was listening to all the conversations. I think my head was hurting but I did not feel it. With all my strength, I was concentrating on their words so I would know what they planned to do with me. To me, it sounded like the driver was afraid and he repeatedly told the man beside me to knock me out again when I woke up. Instead, the man in charge of me put his gun in my mouth again and said, '*Son of a bitch, we will kill you, so do not move and do not even try to shout if you see a police car, or I will kill you right here.'*

"I did not know where they were taking me. I had no time to think of anything except what was happening right then, and that somehow, I must get away from them. There was no time for fear. Every thought was on staying alive. They covered my eyes and tied me with rope. For the rest of the time, I did not see the light of the sun and I was bent over, but I heard all their conversations. They fought a lot between themselves. I heard one of them saying to the other: '*You better behave. The gangsters are not here, but I am the more capable one and I have already killed many people, so you listen to me.*' I was very surprised, after they put me where they took me—I don't know where—when I heard the man say to me: '*I will allow you to see and I'll cut this shit* (the rope) *off your hands—just don't do anything stupid!*'

"Both my hands had been tied with the rope. I had no shoes. The man then said I could have something to eat and drink, but he warned me again not to even think about escaping. To prove his point, he told me to look at him and he pointed his huge automatic gun at me. This went on for a long time. How long, I did not know—forever, it seemed. I lost track of time, but it was days. My captor started to relax more around me when he saw I was not trying to escape. I was so weak. I hadn't eaten or drunk for so long that I eagerly accepted what he gave me and thanked him.

"I began to walk around to get back my strength after being tied in a hard position. I looked around at my surroundings, desperately searching for an escape plan. It was very dark, but I noticed a small door so I asked if I could go to the bathroom. I needed to be able to see what was around me, now that I was no longer blindfolded. He left me untied to do this. I thought the door might lead to the outside. I did not know even where the outside would lead, but I kept this in my mind. After a couple of hours, the man with the big gun told me, '*I am going to the bathroom, so you stay right there. You know I will kill you. You cannot escape from here.*' I was really calm and replied: '*Do not worry; thanks, man, it is so kind of you. Do not worry; Go ahead. I will be here.*'

"Some kind of supernatural peace seemed to come over me. I think I was given special strength and direction. There was no time at all to think about it. I headed directly to the door that I hoped would take me outside. As soon as I heard the bathroom door close, I started to run. Barefoot I ran from that place, not even knowing where I was going. I was just running and not looking back. Physically I was no longer restrained, but in my mind, I still felt the rope around my hands and feet. In a single moment there were so many thoughts. '*Maybe he let me go on purpose so he can shoot me as I escape. Maybe he will come after me and push me in front of a car and make it look like I died in an accident.*' I had to push these thoughts away. Instead, I prayed. I was praying for the entire time I was running. I told God if this escape is meant to be, please help me, and He did. I just ran and ran. I think angels were with me.

"Suddenly I reached a street that looked familiar. I just crossed the road and stood with other people who were waiting for the bus, trying to look like everything was normal. I still felt so much fear, and it seemed like everyone was looking at me. I didn't think about how bad I must look. When I saw the bus coming, I could identify it was coming from the university campus. I did not have shoes. I had so many burns on my face and bruises everywhere on my body, but I felt numb. When I entered the bus, I asked the driver to please take me to the centre where I worked. I told him I just lost everything, and I did not have any money. I held my breath as I waited for his response. Would he turn me away? But he just looked at me and said, 'Come in.'

"I thanked him. My feelings, my thoughts, were moving fast through my brain. I wondered: *'What if one of the killers is on this bus and he is just waiting for me to get off so he can shoot me? Or maybe they are waiting for me outside the police station so they can kill me there.'* I could not turn the thoughts off. The torment in my brain hurt worse than any physical pain. I was so worried about my family. The kidnappers told me they have everything in their control. They knew where we live and what we do, and if I did not cooperate with them something bad would happen to my family. So, I did not try to call anyone. It was a hard decision, but I thought it would be safest to go to my office. It was a good choice. I kept praying.

The week of my kidnapping, my organization hosted an important congress, and all of them quickly realized what must have happened to me. They were all so worried and wrote urgent action letters at the national and international level, asking for help in finding me. When I got back, two people who recognized me identified me and both said: 'It is Jeremias. Thank God you are still alive.' They ran and told all the participants at the conference what they had seen. I just asked one favour of the rest of my colleagues: to leave me alone for a while. That was the first time I had got a chance to look at myself in a mirror. What I saw made everything more real. I cried a lot for a long time. The only thing I remember of the house where I was held is that it was in Guatemala City, la Zona 3, and there was a lot of forest and bushes around."

At this point in the story, Jeremias breaks down. The memories overwhelm him. The reality of what happened and what could have happened is still too acute so we move to a happier place and time, so he can move through his healing.

"SORRY, I CANNOT HANDLE IT ANYMORE ... I WILL TRY ANOTHER TIME ... thank you for understanding," he says, as we begin to talk about a special presentation he is working on for newcomers at one of his schools. It is several months before we talk about the kidnapping again. Jeremias' escape was an incredible feat that took great courage. Most people abducted in Guatemala do not have a similar story.

In the Official Report of the Human Rights Office, Archdiocese of Guatemala, *Guatemala: Never Again!*, the subject of abductions as part of military and government control during and after the massacres is addressed, and attests to the fact that most outcomes are not positive: "Victims of abduction frequently disappeared. According to the testimonies, six out of ten people abducted have still not reappeared A minority of victims reappeared alive (14 percent). One out of every three abduction victims was found dead, often bearing signs of torture. ... This illustrates the frequency with which abductions were used to intimidate or eliminate victims."

After Jeremias returned to work, he was advised he needed to take time off, and make his personal security a priority. He refused, but he lived with incredible fear. Jeremias' fear was not paranoia. It was a reality he carried with him every day, and one of the motivating factors that eventually brought him to Canada. Still, his warrior spirit shone through:

"I was angry and confused," he says. "Even though my bosses told me not to work, I wanted to go back and show no fear. I felt weak. I had no energy, but still I had my courage and desire to fight for social justice. I was inspired and motivated to do so. I told myself I cannot stop because of this act. I know the goal was to weaken us and make us feel stupid. Torture or any type of technique will not work, because even though we will suffer, we know that our ancestors and all the other victims will be with us forever. We dream of a Guatemala in peace and that keeps us going. I could not stop now."

10

Baby Amanda Jasmine

Jeremias was still working with CONFREGUA, providing services to Guatemalan refugees in Mexico, and also providing support to returnees, when his wife became pregnant with their third child. This time the outcome was a difficult one. He was still struggling with the kidnapping and the necessity of hiding his movements. At this time in Guatemala, there was much economic, social, and political unrest. It was the time when the aftermath of the killing of Bishop Juan José Gerardi Conedera was being felt by the people who advocated for human rights. He was a Roman Catholic priest, who had been very active in working with the indigenous Mayan peoples of the country and fighting for their rights.

In 1988, he had been appointed to the government's National Reconciliation Commission to begin the process of accounting for abuses during the civil war. After Bishop Gerardi was attacked in his garage and beaten to death, several Human Rights offices were vandalized, and information related to this work was stolen. All human rights activists were in danger. Jeremias knew this all too well. His wife was discouraged and tired.

"How can we deal with this when you are never home?" she asked him.

Jeremias says they talked and tried to plan how it could work. He made an effort to come home more often. It was a normal pregnancy, even though Soledad was working many hours as an educator and still attending university as a fulltime law student. Jeremias was also busy, but they had a babysitter who helped at home, and their first child, Oscar, at the age of three was already in school. Still, Soledad worked very hard and assumed much of the responsibility for the care of their children. Jeremias continued to travel for work and was at home only about two days each week. Thankfully, he was at home when she went into labour.

He recalls that time: "I was home, and even though it was not her time, I took her to the hospital. But it was too soon, and they sent me home. Then her water broke, and I had to turn around and go back. The actual birth was easy, with little pain, but when my daughter was born, she was taken away for special care because she could not breathe. She had some deformities in her feet and hands, but her heart was the biggest problem. She had to go on a special machine. We could not hold her. It was so hard. She was in the hospital for one month and we took turns staying with her the whole time. I watched her grow and became hopeful. But at three weeks they told us the baby would not live. They asked if we had any other children. When we said *yes*, they said to think about them because she would pass away. We named her Amanda Jasmine.

"I had so many questions, and so did my wife. We both felt so much guilt. We both blamed ourselves for this. It hurt so much. We never held her before she died. Then we took her home to visit family before we buried her in Guatemala City. My sister still pays for her spot to be there. We became a friend to one of the doctors and he encouraged me so much. He told me things would get better. We would be happy again. He told me we could have another baby."

But life had changed for Jeremias and his family. Every day was filled with fear and they continued to grieve for their baby girl, Jasmine. Sometimes, the children were the only thing that kept them going. Jeremias says it was a very dark time, and the children were like a beacon of light.

"Beside my fear and insecurity, I enjoyed my children very much," he says. "Oscar was such a mature little boy. He was always happy to see me coming, and always wanted me to play and be with him. My time with my babies was amazing, but when I came back to reality I was so upset, angry, and annoyed by our living situation. Because of the danger, I did not have a chance to take my children for an ice cream, for example. I could not take the chance. I felt persecuted. I had no freedom to walk, visit my friends, or live a normal life. I had to live in many ways like an actor, because in the daytime I had to be happy and pretend that nothing bothered me. But at night, for a long time I couldn't sleep. I was so sad, angry, and confused. I was terrified someone would hurt the only children I had left and my wife. I did not really care about myself. I was so determined that my family stay safe, I did not worry so much about my own safety.

"Our children brought us joy and happiness, but our family challenge was how, and where, we could hide our children so they could be safe where no one could hurt them. Our concern was always the safety of our children. We both knew my work put everyone in danger, so for many days my wife brought our children with her to her workplace, because we could not always find a babysitter. It was my dream and hope for my children to be in a safe place, to enjoy life, to be free, to have the right to play, and the right of an education. I was still working mostly in Mexico for my protection. My family stayed in Guatemala. I hated to hide. I did not do anything wrong. One day I just decided not to hide anymore, so I went back to Guatemala. But as soon as I got back, the persecution started again. The office where I was working had been ransacked and computers and papers stolen. Everyone there was afraid. Eventually they closed."

11

Hope in the Midst of Danger

After his kidnapping, Jeremias lived in fear that his family would be harmed. He worried constantly. His concerns were not imaginary. His apprehension was valid.

He explains: "There were several attempts to kidnap my wife. There were so many incidents. Paramilitary, hired by the government of Guatemala, were everywhere. When I was involved with Human Rights work, I put my family at risk. One time, my oldest sister, who lived by the main road, had a man in her convenience store talking to her, when my son walked in. The man looked at him and said: 'Hey, Oscar. Where is your dad? I know him; he is my friend.' Oscar told him his dad was working. He saw that the man had a weapon and, even though he was a small boy, he knew to be careful because we had already talked about things like this. He was only about seven years old, but he was aware of the danger. I had already warned him many times to be always watching. He left fast and the man tried to grab him. Oscar ran to my father's house next door and the man tried to get in there. My son jumped through a window and hid in my house which was next door. He told the babysitter and she told me. I told her, 'Margaretta, keep the door locked.'

"One time, my wife was on her way to university and a man approached her on a motor bike. He said 'Soledad, how are you doing? I know your husband, Jeremias. I want to congratulate you. You won something. The office where you can pick it up is open 8-5. I can give you a drive to pick it up.' This confused my wife. She was suspicious right away. She knew she had never entered any contest. She stepped back and told him, 'I know your name. I am a law student and I have your plate number. I memorized your face.' She was walking as she talked. Then she ran and put herself in the group of students. She told others about the danger and asked one to accompany her home on the bus.

"I knew it was not safe anymore. We talked about what we might do. I told her I would talk to some friends to see. I talked to a priest in our community. A few days later, someone came to the home of my father and to my home and knocked on the door. They said they were from the Minister of Justice. They arrived on motor bikes. They called out my name. I didn't know I was talking to my enemy. I took them into our common room, but when Soledad came into the room, she turned white. She refused to talk until they identified themselves. The two men wore gold necklaces and jewelry. One started to laugh. He said, 'What are you afraid of? We worked with genocide cases.' Then he said he was part of the police.

"I said, 'So you are not from the Minister of Justice?' but they ignored my question. They looked around and asked a few more questions about my work. I told them I was not really working right now except for some teaching. They laughed as they left and told us they would let their boss know how cooperative we had been. Soledad said that was the man who stopped her on the motorcycle. She said if we did not leave, they would be back. We left immediately that day. We left everything behind and started to live in different houses. We took only what we could carry. That first night we slept at the priest's house. He helped us find a place. I quit my job but still volunteered. Soledad continued to work and go to school. She wanted to finish because she was in her fourth year and wanted to graduate, but danger was on every corner. And then she found out she was pregnant again."

The fourth child was conceived during a really hard time for Jeremias and Soledad, and this pregnancy brought a new set of fears. After losing Jasmine to what they later found out was a heart condition, Jeremias and Soledad speculated on what could happen. They prayed this baby would be alright. Things were even more difficult for Soledad. Since the kidnapping, Jeremias needed to hide from those who intended to harm him. He still tried to support his family, even though he could not often be with them. He was living in different places for security reasons. Sometimes he went to his office but not often, and he still traveled.

Amazingly, when Soledad went into labour, Jeremias was actually there to welcome his new daughter, born May 20, 2000, exactly one year after he had been kidnapped, on May 20, 1999. And this time his baby girl was healthy. He recalls that day with a smile that brightens his whole face:

"Kira Maya Alejandra Tecu Quiche became our third healthy baby, and she was somehow the resurrection in our family. She seemed to bring us new hope, joy, and happiness. It was a symbolic day, the day she was born. For me, I still couldn't understand a lot of things, like the death of our baby, Jasmine, and the political situation in my country. So Maya was precisely the hope and new life the Tecu Quiche family needed. To me, Maya represented God and the resurrection. She was an angel, a messenger of hope from God, so we could believe again that it will be alright even when we do not have the answers. I held my daughter and felt hope.

"The birth of my youngest daughter changed life for me in many ways. She was an energetic baby, playing a lot. It was hard for my wife. She stayed just one day in the hospital, and when she came home, I could only stay for a few hours. I had to move on the next day. I know that was hard for her, but there was no choice."

Jeremias and his family tried for several months to live as normal a life as possible, but it became increasingly apparent they would not be safe in Guatemala. He did not dare to spend much time at home with his family, and Soledad could not continue looking after three children alone while she worked and attended university. Something had to change if they were to survive as a family. Leaving Guatemala was not a choice Jeremias or his wife wanted to make. They hoped for a safe way to remain in their country.

Jeremias explains this struggle: "My wife and I talked. We agreed the danger was greater than ever. In 1996, the Peace Agreement had been signed, so there was supposed to be peace, but that was still not our reality five years later. I had no choice. I went to the Office of Human Rights and told them about the risks to all my family. I talked to several organizations, but the deputy told me to go to the Ministry of Justice. I spoke to the International Human Right Accompaniment group, and they said I needed to leave the country. I was so thankful I had worked with such kind people, like the representatives from BTS. I asked my friend from Vancouver; she was just like a sister to me. She told me to go. There was no other option but to apply for refugee status.

"A Catholic parish in Washington DC offered refugee status for just me, but I could not accept. I wanted my wife and children with me, so I could be sure of their safety. Then I was told to fill out an application with the Canadian Embassy. It was October 2001by now. We had no passports or anything. They told me it would take one or two years, but some of my friends and colleagues from the International Accompaniment group put on pressure by speaking about our emergency situation. The request even went to the president, Alfonso Portillo, and the new Canadian Ambassador. My friend requested a meeting, and the request was granted. I felt so grateful and so nervous.

"When I met with the Ambassador, I explained my situation to him. I showed him my thick file. I talked to him and asked him to please protect my family. I was asking him to please take me to save my children, even though I did not want to go. He asked lots of questions: 'What type of degree do you have? What kind of work do you do? Do you speak English?' Two hours later, he says, 'Welcome to Canada!' I was crying. I had mixed emotions, but my Canadian friends were so happy."

The dangers for the Tecu family only grew worse. The months before leaving home, nothing was easy. They lived with fears, anger, confusion, and sadness. Jeremias had mixed feelings when he considered leaving. He had been persecuted for years but knowing about the danger that his wife and children, and even his parents and siblings faced, was a burden he did not want to carry. Thanks to caring friends who took the time to make his critical situation known, Jeremias' application to come to Canada was processed quickly. At first, he was told he would have to wait the regular time for an interview, but it was only a day later when he was called.

"I remember that moment," he says. "I shared my story once again and the reason why I was looking for exile for my family. At the time I was crying, and I had a lot of confusion, mixed feelings, anger, sadness. I wanted to leave and go to another country where we could be safe, but I didn't want to leave my home country. The person who was interviewing me asked me why I was applying to come to Fredericton, New Brunswick. He said this province is really poor. Also, he asked me about my profession, and if I spoke any English. I told him: 'No worries; I'm not looking to become rich. My main reason is to have my family in a safe place. And as for my profession, I have faith that I have a lot of skills to offer, and I have two hands and I can work at anything.' I knew people from the BTS network there who would help me, and also some church people. I was a little worried about the language. English? I knew zero English. I didn't speak it or read it or write it, but I could learn. I told him that.

"He looked at me and said we were a young couple with small children who had a long future ahead of us. Then he, like the other man, said, 'Welcome to Canada.'"

Everything moved quickly after that interview. There was a great deal of paperwork, health checks for everyone, then passports and plane tickets. Suddenly it was all too real. It took only one week to have everything in order. Someone from the International Accompaniment group assisted them every step of the way. It all just fell into place. There was not much time for Jeremias to talk to his family, but he did tell everyone except his mother, who was traveling to Rabinal BV. At first, his father said he was sad to be losing another son, but he acknowledged it was good to protect his grandchildren. He understood this was not a move Jeremias was making out of any real choice.

"I will not worry about you," he said to Jeremias. "You are a hard worker, and you will do good work anywhere you are."

Jeremias' sisters and brother all cried when they heard the news. Soledad did not want to leave. She felt she had a good life and a future profession in Guatemala. Even Oscar wanted to stay behind. He refused at first to leave and was very sad, asking if he could live with his aunts.

Jeremias recalls: "I told my wife, and she didn't believe it at first, even when we got our passports. I had the tickets. We were to leave the next day. My wife cried and did not want to come. She said goodbye to her work, and everyone told her to take this opportunity. The day we left was so deeply sad. My family and close friends came to the airport and we could not even talk to them. We had members of International Accompaniments all around the airport, and we were told they would make sure that we were safe until we got to the plane, and warned us to not talk to family or friends for everyone's safety. It was so hard."

12

A New World

On January 31, 2002, the Tecu family left Guatemala. Little Maya was only eight months old. All the way from Guatemala to Miami, USA, they cried. Jeremias tried hard to lift everyone's spirits. He told jokes and eventually got his children to smile, but Soledad did not smile. It was a rough trip in many ways, starting in the airport. The family did not have USA visas. Jeremias had received special permission after his meeting with the Canadian Ambassador, but Jeremias would need to come up with the money. A lady from the airport helped the family secure the pass, and because they had to make their move quickly, there were added costs. Jeremias even had to pay for the baby, and the lady helping them was quite upset by that. She called it a *hussle* and told the immigration officer the baby was too little to run away. They should not charge for her.

"Trying to manoeuvre with three children, Jeremias and Soledad were very tired. At the first stop, they walked through the airport until they found a quiet corner where they could all sit together. The lady accompanying them found a small dark room where they could rest until their next flight. They arrived in Montreal around midnight and it was confusing for the couple. Everything around them was written in French and English. Nothing in Spanish! Jeremias was overwhelmed.

He recalls: "As soon as we got to the Montreal airport, an officer from immigration greeted us by saying, 'Bonjour Madame, Monsieur, Welcome, Bienvenue to Canada.' He asked us questions still speaking in English or French. I did not know what he was saying, so I asked my wife if she understood anything. She shook her head. When I heard 'Bienvenue' I thought maybe it might mean 'welcome' because in Spanish 'welcome' is 'Bienvenido.' It was the only thing that felt even a little bit familiar. The man took us all to one room to sign and stamp our Immigration papers, and then he pointed to a small room. Inside there were boots, jackets, pants, and hats. They were all thick and heavy. I had no idea why we would need any of these. I had never even seen anything like them before. I felt like I was in another world, not just another country.

"I remember he gave us a sack for our baby daughter, and he made signs with his hands to show us to put her inside it. We had a hard time with that. My poor little Maya was crying, and I felt like crying too. But my son and other daughter were really happy wearing big boots and big jackets and trying on pants. All I could think in my head was, 'Oh God, what is happening?'

"I was wearing a sweatshirt and I thought to myself I must be okay like that, because that was a lot of clothes for me. So, I took my gifts, the jacket and boots, and I just carried them in one hand. On my other arm was the baby. The gentleman told us then: 'Hotel.' We left that small storage room, not sure where we were headed, so we just followed. Oh, my God! As soon as I passed through the main glass door and was outside, I suddenly knew why I had those boots and jacket given to me! I told the immigration officer, 'Un momento por favor,' and ran back inside to put everything on. I now understood completely the protocol of the winter jackets and winter boots. It was freezing cold!

"February 1, 2002, we woke up in a hotel room and had a buffet breakfast. I think everyone was in a little bit of shock. It was all so different, and around eight am the officer from Immigration came back for us for our next flight—Montreal to Fredericton, NB. But we sat in the airport and waited and waited. It was storming. Our flight got cancelled many times, and, although it was only a short trip, just over an hour, we did not arrive at the Fredericton airport until midnight that day. While we were flying, a lot of things were going on in my head. For example: *'why is there no light?'* It made me uneasy. Flying for one hour and then another half hour, we were all silent. My children were really tired, but when we got to Fredericton they woke up and were so happy to land.

I was sad and happy at the same time. I was sad to leave my home, but happy because people from the solidarity network group I knew from my country greeted us at the airport. Also, workers from the Multicultural Association of Fredericton were there. Finally, at least we could speak Spanish again!"

13

From a Child's Perspective: Leaving Guatemala

Oscar was only eight years old when the Tecu family left Guatemala. He remembers it well: "I was excited when I first heard we would be moving to a new country," he says. "I even bragged about it to my cousins and my friends, but I don't think I really thought about what it all meant."

Oscar was an active child. He loved playing with his friends and relatives in Guatemala, but he was always aware that danger lurked just outside the safety of those he knew, and even within those confines it was not always good. He says he never really thought about danger in his country when he was there. He knew there were things to watch out for, and he just did what was needed to stay safe and didn't worry about it. But closer to home, he says he did feel afraid around adults and alcohol. He missed his father when he was gone so much, but he was not always happy to see his father either because he knew he would probably be drinking, and drinking would change him also. Oscar worried about the relationship between his parents.

"I remember so much drinking around me when I was a child," he says. "The drinking could often turn into fighting or yelling, and it was not fun to be around this. In Guatemala, the police don't come when there is fighting. People could pretty much do whatever they wanted. It is not like that here in Canada."

Oscar says he does not remember his father being home very much when they lived in Guatemala. He spent most of his time with his mother, aunts, and cousins, and was particularly fond of his maternal grandmother. He says she is the person he still misses the most today. As the days grew closer to leaving, Oscar began to realize the enormity of the coming change. Suddenly, he did not want to leave. The day he entered the airport, the reality hit him; he would not see his relatives in Guatemala for a very long time, or maybe never again. It was overwhelming.

"It was a feeling of deep sadness I had never felt before," Oscar relates in a soft voice, obviously reliving that moment. "I started to cry and could not stop. I begged my dad to let me stay. These were the people I saw every day, and I knew I would not see them again. The feelings inside of me scared me even more. I had never felt such sadness."

Oscar cried through much of the flight. By the time they arrived in Montreal, he had no tears left and started to feel a bit curious.

"I can still remember a particular smell when we got off the plane," he says. "It was new, nothing I'd ever smelled before. It was so cold, and I think now it was the smell that comes with winter. But then it was just strange." Oscar recalls being led to a room where he and his family were given coats, boots, and mittens. It was like arriving in another dimension. He wasn't sure how to put them on and admits there were a few minutes of laughter as he tried to figure it out. When he finally managed it and walked outside to see snow for the first time, he thought he had walked into an enchanted kingdom.

"I was excited when I saw the snow," he admits. "It was almost magical. I'd seen it in movies but now it was real, in front of me, and I thought maybe this won't be so bad after all."

With this thought in mind, Oscar followed his family to a hotel in Montreal where they would spend their first night in Canada before flying on to their new home. The next day, the family arrived in Fredericton. They were taken to a hotel where they stayed for the next few weeks. By now, Oscar was getting curious about this new country and the snow that seemed to be everywhere. He wondered what it would be like to live in snow all the time. It was so different from the hot sun in Guatemala and he could feel a sense of excitement that maybe, just maybe, he would like it.

14

A New Beginning

Jeremias and his family were taken to the Wandlyn Motel in Fredericton, New Brunswick, straight from the plane. They spent the next eight days in a room with three beds. Food was waiting for them. The next day, two smiling women brought in a pot of chicken soup. There were many people and organizations that sponsored Jeremias and his family to come to Canada, but it took a while for them to feel at home.

After arriving in Canada, Jeremias longed to talk to his family in Guatemala to let them know he was safe, and to tell them about this new place, but he knew it was not wise to communicate directly. About a week after he arrived, he sent an email to one of his friends, and asked her to let his parents know he and his family had arrived safely in Canada. It was almost five more years before he ventured to call them directly by telephone.

After spending a week in the hotel, Jeremias started to look at apartments where they could live. He settled on a two-bedroom one on Biggs Street in Fredericton. It was not really big enough for a family of five, and his wife did not like it, but Jeremias said it was all they could afford. He thought it was beautiful, and his children were very happy to have a new home. This meant the two oldest children could now start school, even though they did not yet speak English. Oscar and Mayte started school one week after the family moved to their new home. Oscar went to Forest Hill Elementary and Mayte, now five years old, went to Liverpool Elementary School, which housed children from Kindergarten to grade three. The two schools were only a few blocks from each other, and the children eventually traveled together by school bus, which they loved.

However, Jeremias did not know about the school bus in the beginning, and walked for almost 30 minutes all the way through the ice and snow for the first week, to make sure the children could have the advantage of education in this new country. It was times like this Jeremias wished for the warmth of his country of birth and questioned his decision to come to such a cold place. Had he been able to communicate in English, he might have been spared this experience.

Arriving in Canada in the middle of winter, it was the first experience that included ice and snow for Jeremias and his family. He was sure they must have arrived in Iceland. By summer, he felt much more at home. Canadian friends invited the Tecu family on outings and swimming. Jeremias began to see Canada as a new paradise. By their first Christmas in Canada, the family felt much more at home, even though for Jeremias it was a bigger adjustment.

He explains: "It was really hard for me. I tried to go along with the new ways, but in Guatemala we have a lot of traditions around Christmas. It is not about presents. It is about being together with all the family, siblings, and relatives, and I felt that I had lost all of them. I missed the smell of the decorations. At home, they were real, not fake. They were made from our trees and flowers. I missed the smell of the traditional food. I missed my mother's cooking and, even though I tried to bring happiness to my children, I cried after they went to bed that first Christmas in Canada. It was a really tough experience."

Adjusting to Canadian food in general was another hurdle. This took time for the Tecu family, but eventually they found a way to compromise their taste buds. Jeremias recalls his excitement at a presentation he was doing for work. He saw there was a buffet that included beans, one of the staple foods in Guatemala. His family also attended.

"We were all so happy when we saw the food," he says. "It was a huge table, and in between the other main dishes there were beans. My children and I were so happy to help ourselves to the beautiful beans. But, oh my goodness, when we started eating them, those beans were sweet! We never expected those beans to be sweet. We never ate sweet beans before! My children didn't like it and I didn't like it either, but we were trying to be polite. When I think about it now, it makes me laugh.

It was hard to adapt our diet. Mostly, we cooked rice and noodles. Bread didn't really work. When we sent our children sandwiches for school lunch they just came back, because no one was used to eating this. So, we solved the problem. We sent *dobladas*, made from corn flour, fried with cheese inside, a type of the *samosas* that many people in Fredericton eat. That was different and they loved it. It was hard to find our traditional foods, or even close to what we used to eat, even the fruits and vegetables, and especially the tortillas."

Jeremias was determined to learn English. He remembered how hard it had been to learn Spanish as a child after only speaking Achi, but still he learned. He knew he could do it, but it was not easy. He attended classes faithfully and often felt very frustrated. He says learning English was much harder than learning Spanish.

He explains: "English was definitely one of the hardest things about coming to Canada. When I first went to the group to learn, I thought everyone already knew how to speak English, because they were having conversations. I did not realize many of them were not speaking English either. I felt alone with zero English, but still I did my best and it was good. I connected immediately with the class and made friends. One of them from Iran spoke to me in Persian and I spoke in Spanish. I don't know what we were both talking about, but both of us talked anyway and at the end we both laughed a lot. I don't know what he got from me and I don't know if I gave him the answer to what he was talking about, but after that I did not feel so alone."

Dealing with memories of times and people in Guatemala did not come so easily. As Jeremias settled into a new life in a country where he felt safe, he had more time to think about the past and the pain. Flashbacks, even though he did not know then what they were called, became more prevalent and disturbing. Sometimes in the beginning he used alcohol again to cope, but he also allowed himself to feel the pain, and began to turn to physical activities like running to get through.

He explains: "I cried when I needed to cry. I knew my story was one of hundreds of human beings who lived during the time of the violence in Guatemala. I realized those soldiers who hurt my people were part of the government that tried to destroy my life. They were no longer around me, but they took my human wellbeing away from me. It was so hard to think and cope with all my fears. Things came to my mind even when I did not invite them. At first, I drank, but I would also pray. Then I started to practice sports instead of drinking. It was not just the memories. It is so difficult to adjust to a new culture. For me, being here in this country I knew I was safe, but it also meant a huge part of my life was missing. Sometimes I feel like I'm here physically, but in my spirit I'm back in Guatemala beside my people, working and being inspired by their struggles."

Jeremias began to adapt to his new life and slowly learned the new language, but he was still not ready to resume roles similar to those he had carried out in his birth country. Even though he was a university graduate, his first job was ironically at the University of New Brunswick as a janitor. He was grateful for the work and did his best.

"I started to work part time as a janitor at UNB," he says. "But I was very scared about making mistakes. I cried many times because I had never done this type of job before, and I did not know how to ask many questions. I just tried my best. After I would finish, I would come back home and not show this sadness. I just showed happiness to my children, so they would not be upset. Then I learned how to paint houses. I liked this work much more. Summertime was a wonderful time to work. I started work at 6 am and continued until 10 pm, because in summer the days are longer, and I enjoyed it very much."

The Multicultural Association of Fredericton (MCAF) played such an important part in the lives of the Tecu family that Jeremias was proud to be able to give something back. Not only had the MCAF hosted his family when they arrived in Canada, they provided the orientation that taught them how the system works regarding life skills and employment, cultures, and daily living. They provided the initial opportunity to learn English through their ESL classes. Jeremias gained confidence to push further and decided to challenge himself by enrolling in classes at Saint Thomas University. He wanted to learn more about political sciences and human rights and improve his English through courses that would enhance the degree he received in Guatemala. He had been in Canada only a few months before he requested to volunteer for the MCAF at their Rainbow of Cultures Summer Camp.

"I already had a lot of experiences working with children, youth and people of all ages," he says. "But in this first experience I felt helpless because of the language. I wanted so badly to play, sing, and have fun but no one understood me. It made me sad."

In September of that same year, the MCAF was looking for someone who could drive and facilitate the newcomer children and youth program. One of Jeremias' host volunteers told him he should apply, so he decided to try again. The MCAF employment counsellor helped him to develop a resume. When he dropped it off at the main office, he was called for an interview almost immediately. He was so determined to get the job he fought off his nervousness, and simply answered all the questions according to his previous work experiences.

"What can you contribute to help newcomer children adjust to Canadian culture?" he was asked.

He recalls there were three people in the room, two women and one man. They looked friendly, especially the women. The man was not so friendly.

"He kept asking me what I was going to do to accomplish this," Jeremias says. "I did not know the word *accomplish* so I kept asking him to repeat it in a different way, but I did not feel he was pleased."

The man worked with the government, according to Jeremias, and didn't seem convinced he would be capable of the job.

"I always put my clients first," Jeremias told the interviewers, looking directly at the man. "I think about their happiness."

After the interview he felt good, but also wondered if he was ready because of the language issue. His English was still very limited, so he was not really sure he was the best choice.

"But that same day I was told I would probably get the job," he says.

Two days later, the director, Lisa Bamford, stopped him on his way to English class. He had his baby daughter, Maya, with him. She congratulated him. He had the job!

"I went to my English class, but at break time I met my wife and told her," he says. "We were both so happy. It felt like life was finally going in the right direction."

Jeremias says that was one of his happiest moments in Canada, but after a couple of weeks he became quite frustrated. He had lots of good ideas and wanted to plan activities, but the language was a barrier. He thought maybe someone else, someone more qualified with good English, should have the job after all, so he decided to tell the director they might have made a mistake by hiring him. But the director did not agree. She encouraged Jeremias to be patient with himself and continue working on his English. She told him he was doing a good job!

"I really appreciated that comment from my director," he says. "From that moment on I just kept trying. I thanked her for her trust in me and promised to do the best job I could do, and it was amazing. Little by little it all came together, and we did many projects and I even learned how to have fun in winter."

He says one of his most outstanding memories that first year with MCAF took place in the winter during *Winter Fest*. They took the children and youth sledding. At first it was easy and fun, but after only a few minutes everyone was freezing from the cold. Jeremias was not sure what to do, because he was not used to playing any winter sports. In desperation, he looked around. He looked at the field in front of him. It was empty and shiny from the snow, but it was still an empty field. *'What about soccer?'* he thought to himself as he went to find some plastic bags. He quickly put one inside the other, filled them with snow to make a ball—a soccer ball—and invited the newcomer children and youth to their first game of snow soccer.

"It was so much fun," he says with a smile that brightens his face. "Everyone had fun, but it was not too easy. I think the next day everyone had bruises—green or black areas on our bodies that told us this was not a good way to play soccer, but it worked for us on that cold day. A lot of these kids came from warm countries like me and standing around in the cold was not a fun experience. Most of us had never heard of hockey. Kids were from the Congo, Latin America, Afghanistan, African countries. Soccer was a common language, even in the snow."

15

Settling in for Oscar

After Oscar started attending school, he remembers feeling a bit nervous but also excited. He knew everyone would be speaking English and he could only speak Spanish.

"I think there were not as many kids from other countries around back then," he says. "When the teacher said my name, all the other kids gathered to welcome me. I felt excited, like a celebrity. No one seemed to care that I was the only one there with brown skin. Colour didn't seem to matter, and I never saw it being a problem throughout school for the most part, especially in elementary school."

Oscar says it was probably much easier to integrate as an eight-year-old. He believes it is much harder for teenagers and adults. He also picked up English easier than some, and was determined to do his best to fit in.

"I realize I will always be a minority," he says. "But this has not been a problem for me because I am active and make friends easily. In fact, all my best friends growing up were born in Canada. I had one boy from South America who mentored me for a while, but I usually hung out with kids from Fredericton."

It did not take long to embrace Fredericton as home. Oscar became involved at the Fredericton Multicultural Association where his father was employed. He became active in the youth group and played soccer. But making music was his favourite pastime and music soon became his number one love.

"The music was always there," he says. "Even in Guatemala I loved music, but it was when I was 14 and took guitar lessons that music really became important. I worked three months at Burger King when I was 14 years old, just so I could buy an electric guitar."

Today, Oscar, in his mid-20s, is playing in a band and has even recorded his own music. Recording his CD was a huge project, where he provided all musical accompaniments: guitars, bass, drums, vocals, keyboard and even wrote the music. Oscar graduated from Fredericton High School in 2011 and is now attending university. Music is still his first love and experimenting with analog equipment gave him the idea for a unique sound.

On June 5, 2020, Oscar debuted as "lil Omar" with his first solo album through Bandcamp after several years of success with Chillteens, the band he founded in 2015 (and in which his little sister also performs). Chillteens is a four-piece band featuring psychedelic rock with elements of jazz and R&B. Up until the beginning of the COVID-19 pandemic, which put a stop to all live performances, Oscar and his band mates in Chillteens had been working on writing a new album, but that project had to be put on hold.

Releasing a solo album was a very happy accomplishment for Oscar, but it was also a sad day according to his interview with the *Elephant Journal*: "You see, while I've been at home for the past three months making and finishing my Toddler Country record, current events in the world and in my own personal life have been draining me emotionally. Today, I've been trying to feel excited and proud of the work I've done. I am excited. I do feel proud. But along with that comes a great amount of sadness and guilt. Sadness for my black, indigenous, and coloured brothers and sisters."

In reference to the killing of black Americans by police in the United States, he made his position clear: "My hopes are that with these current events and online protesting, we're also able to stand up to our racist family, friends, bosses, and coworkers. Challenge those who need to be challenged. Go further than posting a black square on your Instagram. Donate to the cause. Get informed. Support artists of colour. It is a privilege to educate yourself about racism instead of experiencing it."

To back his words, Oscar announced he would be donating half of the profits from this solo album on Bandcamp to the Canadian Civil Liberties Association.

16

Fitting In

Working for the MCAF brought Jeremias much satisfaction. He began by helping newcomers with their settlement and integration into Canada, a process he knew well. It was the same kind of work he had been doing in Guatemala, and he felt happy to do his part to help refugees and contribute to his new country, Canada, in a meaningful way. After only a couple of months with MCAF, Jeremias was asked to attend the Canadian Council for Refugees (CCR) conference for the first time. He was apprehensive and excited all at once. There he met many refugees from countries throughout the world, and they often had similar stories and similar experiences. Some of the similarities matched his own.

In the fall of 2003, he was elected as a member of the executive committee for the CCR and continued in this role until 2011. That meant he would attend three conferences and three working groups each year. The mandate was to meet the needs of refugees more effectively, and it was a cause Jeremias passionately pursued. He saw it as an important mission because the recommendations that would come out of the meetings would be presented to MPs in the House of Commons. He hoped this would mean positive changes for all refugees in Canada.

"It is good to bring groups of people here to a safer country, but all human beings have personal needs and rights, and for refugees especially, mental health can be complicated with issues like student's special needs and so much more," he explains. "I knew firsthand the resources too often are not available to meet these needs, so I hoped to make a difference."

Jeremias was concerned about what he called "modern day slavery." He knew people from other countries were being illegally trafficked on a regular basis in Canada, but he despaired that not enough attention was being given to the abuses suffered "legally." He considered the plight of temporary foreign workers often fit into this category. Truck drivers, for example, who might bring fruits and vegetables from other countries, could be on the road for three weeks each month and only spend a few days at home. They had no health care, no services, no rights. This frequently applied to *nannies* brought from other countries as well. They often received no pay but worked long hours for food and shelter only. They could not complain because they would be deported, and for most, living this way as a "modern day slave" was still better than the life they had left behind.

"Under the Harper government, anyone who wanted to be a permanent resident in Canada needed to write a test, but this test was in English," Jeremias says. "Most who wanted to come to Canada knew little or no English; they could never pass a test like this. That, to me, is a violation of human rights."

By this time, Jeremias' wife was working part time in a daycare and her English was greatly improved. The couple moved to downtown Fredericton and the children transferred to Connaught Street School. Work was within walking distance for both of them.

In 2005, the Tecu family moved back to Biggs Street so they could have a co-op house. Now Oscar was ready for Albert Street Middle School, and Maya was preparing to go to the French school, Ecole Ste. Anne, so she could be truly considered bilingual in the province of New Brunswick. The family had already applied for Canadian citizenship. In November 2006, the Tecu family was granted its request. The ceremony took place in the centre attached to Maya's school and was similar to a graduation ceremony. Newcomers to Canada were called upon by families to receive their certificates, the paper that would declare them to be true Canadians. Jeremias recalls that there were people from many different countries, and most were quite excited.

"I think there were probably 70 people there," he says. "I had mixed feelings because my heart was still very much in Guatemala, but I was also proud and thankful to be blessed to come to a safe country like Canada."

Jeremias remembers several officials at the ceremony: a judge, a few representatives from Immigration Canada and other government departments, and an RCMP officer dressed in his red uniform and black boots. He says there were also many of his friends from MCAF and BTS there to celebrate with him, and their excitement fueled his own during this experience.

"They were so happy for me and they brought all of us presents and flowers," Jeremias says. "My children didn't really know what was going on, but they were happy to get the presents and share everyone else's enthusiasm."

After the ceremony, one of Jeremias' colleagues had a barbecue for the Tecu family. There was a special cake to mark the occasion and this was a big hit with the children. Oscar says he wasn't really sure what the certificate was for, but he was happy to have a day off from school to have so much fun. For Jeremias, the main significance of the Certificate of Citizenship was that he could now have a voice in the federal election; he could now vote.

Jeremias enjoyed the variety in his role as settlement worker, but it was far from a 9-to-5 job. Sometimes, the phone would ring at 1 am asking him to take a sick child to the hospital, or he might be called at any hour to mediate a family conflict. The police would also call him to discuss various matters.

"This job was more complex than working as a child and youth facilitator," he explains. "Being a settlement worker, you have to handle many cases, taking care of new arrivals. Not only do you work with the families as an interpreter, but you might also have to work with a judge, a lawyer, a pastor, a doctor, or some other advisor. There were only two settlement workers back then to handle all the new people coming. Today there are five settlement workers at MCAF. It was a lot of work, but I loved it from the minute I started."

"I once got several calls from a young pregnant mother who spoke no English," he recalls. "She and the father were scared and just needed reassurance they would be safe. We used interpreters from the centre, so it took a lot of time."

Finding interpreters can be difficult. Most languages represented in the community of newcomers to Fredericton have someone who can take on that task, but not always. Jeremias says he once needed one for a woman from Sudan facing surgery. He had to initially Skype with someone from Edmonton. Then that person had to be flown in, so the client would fully understand the consent process required before surgery could proceed.

Jeremias worked hard in this position until September 2009, and then MCAF opened a position for a settlement worker in schools (SWIS). He had always loved working with youth, so he applied and was hired. He has been working there ever since. As a settlement worker, Jeremias had been making sure all government-assisted refugee families met their initial settlement needs, but now as a settlement worker in schools, the mandate was more complex and consisted of four components: to help newcomer children and youth in schools understand the education system in Canada; to plan and deliver programs as part of the children's successful social and educational integration; to act as liaison and support for newcomer parents with school teachers and administrators; and, to ensure school staff understand cultural differences in order to promote cultural competency. This meant Jeremias would present several training and information sessions, in addition to his hands-on work with clients. It was a tall order. Jeremias was soon working 60-70 hours per week, sometimes more!

"I was already familiar with the problems," he says. "The children make mistakes because they do not understand, and the parents do not understand. They already have their own stresses. I was the parent of children new to Canada also, so I thought maybe I could help solve some of these problems."

Jeremias loved his new role, but too often he felt frustrated with the challenges faced by the children who were trying to find their way in an unfamiliar country. The lack of cultural sensitivity from those with power never failed to make him sad, and the lack of appropriate mental health services became glaringly evident. Sometimes a simple misunderstanding could turn ugly. A student, not understanding the language or social customs, might try to do something to fit in, or might refuse to participate. But the consequence of such acts, even if they started as something trivial, could escalate to the point where the police might get involved. Jeremias says many of the students are coming from war-torn countries and have PTSD, but these facts are seldom considered.

"I remember a teenaged boy from Liberia, Africa, who came to Fredericton with his father, two of his sisters, and a stepmother," he recalls. "He seemed tired, but he was willing to participate in our events at the centre. He said he wanted a job, and I helped him get one at a local meat market. He worked there part time, and also attended fulltime classes at the Fredericton High School (FHS). It seemed like he was settling in well. Then something happened at FHS. He was caught using his cell phone during class time, and the vice principal took him to his office. It turned into a traumatic experience. The boy said he was only putting the phone away. This young fellow came from a war-torn country. He had seen so much genocide and torture. I was concerned the administration never took this into consideration when they decided to discipline him. When he was told to leave the office and leave his cell phone, he refused and sat down. The VP tried to push him out the door and threatened to call the police. Can you imagine what this young man was thinking and feeling?

"The policewoman came and tried to take the student's hand. He pushed her back and refused to leave. He told her the VP was lying. They called for backup. They put him on the floor, stepped on him and put him in a choke hold and took him to the lockup. They never contacted the parents or me. When he was released, he was so sad, angry and confused. He called me in tears. The second day, I set up an appointment with the VP. I did not even think to consult with my boss, I was so angry. But everything changed when the door opened, and I was called by my name. The VP knew me. I said: 'Do you even know this student?' He said 'No,' so I explained this boy's situation. This phone was all he had. He was the only son of a mother who did not make it out of the refugee camp. He still used the phone to check on his mom. I learned a lot from the boy when I spoke to him again later that day. I found out how hard he was working. His story connected with me. He was not selfish; he was kind and respectful. He was sending money to his mother. The punishment was to kick him out of school for six months. I asked the VP to go to the police station to get rid of that charge. The student did not touch the VP or the police. I ripped up the paper telling the boy he was expelled from school."

Jeremias says the vice principal was surprised by the emotion he was showing, but he was listening.

"I want you to call that student to come back tomorrow or I call Human Rights," he told the school administrator.

Jeremias' words moved the vice principal. He was willing to give the student a chance, and that chance is one of Jeremias' success stories. The young man ended up graduating and is now married and lives in Edmonton. This story ended well, but it could have had a completely different ending. Stories like this, ones with happy endings, still buoy Jeremias up, when he feels himself sinking in a world where racism and intolerance never completely disappear. To see youth succeed against the odds gives him the energy he needs to keep working. Jeremias is a constant 'cheerleader'. If a student is told they will be lucky if they even graduate, he tells them they can be successful professionals in the future, as long as they work hard and believe in themselves.

He remembers a brother and sister from Nepal, who had been told by a guidance counselor that they had a very poor chance of making it through school. Both were failing Math and English. Jeremias prayed and contacted Frontier College for tutors. He asked for volunteers because there was no money to pay anyone. His prayer was answered. The youth started meeting with tutors three hours each day, six days per week. Things slowly started to change. The teachers said they could see a difference. Jeremias got them into summer school. He found them a sponsor. They both graduated and were awarded as outstanding students for their hard work, which they accomplished in two years. Their happiness could hardly be contained. The young man eventually graduated from the Engineering program at the University of New Brunswick. The young woman completed a business program at the same university. The whole family is proud but not prouder than Jeremias, who often loves to share this story.

Jeremias is sometimes personally triggered by the stories of his clients. He often feels discouraged. But he has a routine that helps him stay focused. He explains:

"I pray most of the time when I have the feeling that I cannot handle a situation. I just turn around and change the activity or go for a 'reflection walk.' I always come back with a different and positive point of view. I also try all the time to let go of any anger or resentment. I seek to be happy, and project that in many ways to make my clients happy. But I admit, sometimes I do have to fake it to keep going, and it is very hard when I see my clients suffering. I feel their pain, too."

Jeremias believes that there needs to be some changes to help refugees coming to North America. He wants people in Canada to try to understand *why* refugees come in the first place. He says open-mindedness and patience from Canadians is vitally important in creating successful transitions for newcomers.

"If you do not understand the newcomer, never be afraid, because we are human beings who in many cases never choose to leave our home," he says. "It is a frightening journey, and many of us had to make sacrifices and face fear, not knowing what to expect. We are not the enemy."

Today, Jeremias continues to enjoy his work in the schools. He feels he has developed expertise in presenting to community partners as well as to the students, families. and staff for all grades: K-Elementary, Middle and High School. Sometimes, he is also asked to speak at university events. He especially likes presenting during Black History Month, talking about the atrocities that the African descendants have suffered. He says he feels the pain of these brothers and sisters also. He tries to be part of the solution, the change that speaks out against any kind of discrimination.

"The future is here, and change is you and me," he says. "Nobody else has the responsibility to change the world and make it a better place to live. We are all responsible."

17

Hints of Racism

Oscar says that being in Canada is like being in Heaven for him. He has always felt accepted by the people around him. He would not want to go back to Guatemala to live, even though he would like to see some of his relatives, especially his grandmother.

"It is a corrupt place and very dangerous," he says. "And I have memories that are good, but I also have memories that are bad, especially when drinking was involved. Things improved so much in Canada."

Even though Oscar says he only experienced occasional brief uneasiness from racist jokes later in his teen years, he never really saw overt racism aimed directly at him until more recently, and this was a game-changer.

He explains: "I just got off work at the Crown Plaza Hotel around three am, so some friends and I went to a McDonald's we knew was open 24/7 to get something to eat. After we sat down, I noticed a guy sitting at another table staring at me. I was the only person in the place who was obviously not white, and when he got up and started walking towards me, I felt scared. He started calling me a Mexican and went on about how all Mexicans should get out of the country, and he knew how they treated their children and on and on. It was surreal. I felt an impulse to fight, but when I looked into his eyes, I saw he was high so I just sat down. Other people got him to leave. He went outside and started walking up to an Asian couple who were standing next door. I felt sick inside. I was shaken."

For Oscar, this triggered something he had not thought about in a long time. He did look different. He *was* different, and no matter how well he might fit in with the people in his circle, he would always be part of the minority in this city and in this country. Suddenly he realized this was a truth, and one that carries some responsibility. Those racist jokes or slurs aimed at him or a friend that he has brushed off and ignored were no longer acceptable. So even though, as a very peaceloving individual, he never wanted to confront situations, he knew he must now speak up. He would allow himself to be uncomfortable, while calmly speaking his truth. And, as he sees more examples of racism in the news, his resolve grows stronger to help. Racism in any form is not acceptable.

18

Breaking the Silence in Canada

Long before Jeremias and his family arrived in Canada, he became friends with some people from Canada who ended up being his main supporters—the people from Breaking the Silence (BTS). He needed to be accompanied at work for five years as an important measure of protection, beginning even before arriving in Canada. They were there for him and continued to be.

Jeremias explains the accompaniment process: "When you are in an environment that is insecure and dangerous, and it is the government that backs this, no one can be sure of complete freedom or protection. Guatemala has one of the most beautiful constitutions in Latin America, but it is just a book that only comes out when it is time to show off to other countries. They say it is a democracy, but this is not true when only two or three own the land and are responsible for the killing. That is why we need international accompaniment. We need these people to be with us to make sure we are safe, people like those from BTS. It saves lives. They try to promote human rights."

When Jeremias and his family arrived in Fredericton it was BTS, along with members of the local multicultural association, who were waiting at the airport to welcome them. For Jeremias, it provided a measure of comfort to be welcomed by people who had already helped him so much, and people who could also speak Spanish. Before leaving Guatemala, Jeremias vowed he was not ever again going to speak about what was happening there, nor be involved in any kind of activism that could put him or his family at risk. But he felt a connection to BTS, and he was grateful for what they did for him, so when they asked him to come to one of their meetings, he could not refuse. Only two weeks after his arrival, Jeremias travelled to Tatamagouche in Nova Scotia, a three-hour trip by car, where he was asked to speak. That initiated a new journey of involvement with BTS for him, but it was a difficult new beginning.

He recalls: "I could hardly speak. I said I was really sad. I did not want to talk about it, but I needed to talk about it. Then I told everyone I was sorry, but I had to go. I was crying. I left to get a glass of water, and I got a new resolve. I knew my words were the words of many people who had died, and I needed to go back and talk. So I did. I cried, but I was ready. I started to talk about it, though I never looked at anyone. The second day I was told everyone was crying in the room. I did not notice because I was not looking. It was powerful for me and for the others, I think. It was the first time I had exposed myself. I felt naked before the community. It was like taking a shower and washing out what I had carried in me for 30 years."

BTS kept in contact with Jeremias, and gradually he began to get involved and speak in other places: Prince Edward Island; Miramichi, New Brunswick; Quebec; Toronto; and at the Canadian Council for Refugees, where he sat on the board as a director. There was no way Jeremias could stop trying to speak out. He was an advocate at heart and began to speak more often. Eventually, he became the Fredericton Coordinator for BTS. Raising money to help the organization with its work was part of his mandate, so he helped organize a yearly event to do so. *Noche Latina* soon became an annual evening of Latino food and music hosted by the Maritime-Guatemala Breaking the Silence Network and co-hosted by the Multicultural Association of Fredericton (where Jeremias still works today). The evening offers a traditional Guatemalan meal combined with Latin rhythms. People from all cultures are quick to join in the dancing. There is also a silent auction, with unique items from Latin America as well as donations from local merchants and supportive Fredericton residents. This event is usually held yearly in February in Fredericton and tickets are always sold out. Proceeds go to support ongoing solidarity work in Guatemala and the MCAF Newcomer Scholarship Fund. Promoting education for youth is important to Jeremias. He says BTS provides a valuable service, and their work today is more important than ever.

"The promotion of human rights and social justice is important on any level," he says. "But even more important is to be a voice for the people who have no voice. We need to understand what is normal, and we need people here in Canada to understand what has been normal for some of us. Maybe for me to see a person cut in pieces was part of my normal life in Guatemala, but in Canada it is not normal, and I know this. In a culture of quietness, we prepare our mind to be normal, but it is *not* normal. I know because I am a survivor, and people from BTS try to help us and everyone else understands this, except for the mental health system. They do not seem to understand."

19

First Trip Back to Guatemala

In the spring of 2009, Jeremias was selected from many other candidates to represent Canada in an international conference focused on immigration issues. It was to be held in Guatemala in July. He received the invitation from Citizenship and Immigration Canada (CIC) through the CCR. At first, he was excited. After all, it had been more than seven years since he had seen his relatives in Guatemala, and this trip would give him an opportunity to do so. In addition, he cared greatly about the people in his birth country and hoped by going there he could make some small but positive contribution.

On the other hand, he knew the fears that he kept at bay living safely in Canada would gain control, and plague him as soon as he set foot on the plane. He wondered if he could even concentrate at the conference, once he was actually back in his country, which was still very much controlled by a corrupt system and its militant enforcers. He booked his ticket for two weeks (one week for the conference and one week to spend with his family), but he wasn't sure if he would make it through the first day. The first hitch on the trip took place at the Toronto International Airport. Jeremias felt both fear and frustration when he was singled out by the customs officers.

"They kept calling me Juan Manuel Tecu," he says. "And I kept telling them it was not my name and showing them my passport." For Jeremias, this was one of his greatest fears. "They were convinced I was someone else, someone who I think was not allowed into the country. I kept saying, 'My name is Juan Jeremias Tecu Quisque.' But they did not listen, and no one would tell me what was going on. I was really sad, upset, and angry. After several hours, I told them if they did not believe me, they could talk to CIC and the CCR. They would tell them the truth about me.

"Eventually they let me go, but by the time I reached my gate the plane had already left. Fortunately, the company where I bought my airplane ticket was able to give me another one to connect to the USA. But I would have to spend a night in the USA before leaving the next day for Guatemala. Because of this, I missed one day of the conference and my luggage did not arrive for four days. When I arrived in Guatemala airport, another challenging situation was in front of me. Since I was representing Canada in this important conference, the Guatemalan government was providing transportation from the airport to the conference hotel. But the first thing I noticed was that most of the people who welcomed us were carrying guns or other weapons. There was no way I could trust these people. I had been kidnapped by pretty much the same type of people!

"Before leaving Canada, I had made arrangements to meet with our BTS Guatemala representatives. These were people I could trust, the people who made sure I made it safely out of Guatemala in the first place. Thank God, the same woman who made all those arrangements was there with a cab. I went with her and that's when I felt safe, and it was the first time in hours I knew I could talk with freedom, and get out all the frustration I had felt since I left home for Guatemala City. It had not turned out to be such a pleasant trip, and I was to face further disappointment with my plans to see my family."

Jeremias was advised it would not be safe for him to spend a week with his family. After so long with no contact, he was saddened by this news. He was told it would not be wise to go anywhere close to their homes, because this would put them all at risk. He was reminded that the risk was not all political. Even organized crime could prey on a vulnerable relative if they thought there was someone there from a 'rich country' like Canada, who could pay a ransom to get them back from a kidnapping. If Jeremias attended the conference, kept a low profile, and stayed mostly in the hotel, he would probably be safe, but visiting his family would certainly be a high risk for all of them. Jeremias was very sad to be so close to his family but unable to visit, but he did not want to do anything to put their lives at risk. He longed to be able to visit familiar places, but he decided he would concentrate on the conference.

"The conference was a full week," he explains. "This experience was very healing and productive at the same time. While I was there, I did not think of anything else. Everyone was sharing a lot of experiences at the national and international level. They were long full days. During the day, it appeared the hotel was safe with many security personnel from the national government. At night, all through the nights, you could hear them in the hallways, walking all night. I couldn't sleep in peace. I was afraid and felt a lot of frustration.

"At the conference I was so tired after a few days. I want-ed to visit home. I wanted to surprise my relatives, but always there was great fear, and it kept me from my dreams. I did pretty much nothing, just being part of the conference, helping out with the different workshops, and meeting people who worked with immigrants in Guatemala. I spent the entire week in the hotel. The government of Guatemala gave all participants a tour in and around Guatemala City, but I was afraid to go out, so I decided to stay inside. Only on the last night of the conference did I venture out to be with our BTS representative in Guatemala.

"On the next day, I had a special surprise. I met secretly with my father, mother, brother, and sisters. That day was a special blessing. After such a challenging week, I finally got to meet my family. It had been so many years hearing nothing from them. There was a lot of emotion, a lot of sadness, too. They did not believe that I was really there."

Jeremias had mixed feelings about returning to Canada. He felt sad to be leaving Guatemala again, but he missed his family in Canada. He wanted to be able to challenge his fears and visit Guatemala freely, but he knew he could not at this time, and this left him feeling more frustrated and sadder than before.

"I remember asking myself *why?*" he says. "*Why* are there such injustices and violations of my right to belong to my birthplace with my relatives?"

For Jeremias, the flight back was without incident, but he wept a great deal along the way. Confusion about how little things had changed in his country dogged every thought. Only when he arrived in Fredericton and saw his children and his wife did he feel a measure of comfort. As he hugged them, he cried again and promised never again to leave them alone. For the next few days, he often felt like he was disconnected from his body.

He explains: "I would feel connected and disconnected with my spirit—like part of me was still in Guatemala sometimes. Reconnecting to that reality was hard. I was not sure where I belonged, and it made me sad. It was almost a shock again to connect to that culture of danger, to be at risk, something I had never experienced for many years. The culture of violence was so different from my experience since coming to Canada. Here I could live a normal life, enjoy running for exercise and pleasure. There, running was associated for me with death and escape. I could not help but appreciate the peace and freedom of where I live now. I knew I was blessed to live in Canada in this context of peace."

20

Grim Reality

In the spring of 2013, Jeremias asked me to meet with him. I assumed he was ready to tell more of his story and looked forward to our reunion, since it had been several weeks since we last got together. I knew Jeremias needed some space and time to process. It wasn't unusual that it could take weeks, sometimes as long as three or four months, before he would be ready. I tried to follow his lead. But this time he sounded different and as soon as I saw him, I could tell something was bothering him. "What's wrong?" I asked. He replied with a story.

"My friend Daniel, we were in school together in Instituto Indigena Santiago La Salle in Guatemala City. The last time I talked to him we were in his community in Santa Eulalia. It was 1997 or 1998, and he was a teacher but also a great community leader and activist. I was involved in community work there, providing some training. We supported some of the community projects. At the time there was not a hydroelectric plant going in, but there was talk about it. Later when it came, it was destroying the water for many communities, so the leaders from the communities were trying to get a consultation to have this changed. The protests were very peaceful in the beginning, but the responses were not always so peaceful. Daniel was one of the people protesting this, and that is why he is now dead."

Jeremias received news of the murder of Daniel Pedro Mateo only days before. He could not sleep and knew he must talk about it. That is why he called me. He was gripped again by the tentacles of anguish that had shackled him when he still lived in Central America, but this time he trusted someone enough to share his grief. He showed me the announcement from April 18, 2013, in the *Upside Down World* (a news and analysis outlet covering social movements and politics in Latin America):

On April 16, 2013, the body of Qanjob'al community activist Daniel Pedro Mateo was found murdered in Santa Eulalia, Huehuetenango, Guatemala. He had been kidnapped for 12 days and his body showed signs of torture.

Daniel, a founder of the community radio station Snuq Jolom Konob, disappeared on Sunday, April 7th in the village of El Quetzal, Huehuetenango, on his way to host a workshop on Indigenous rights in the community of Santa Cruz Barillas. His family was contacted by kidnappers and demanded a ransom of Q150,000 in return for his safety. Despite the efforts of his family and community to gather money to pay the ransom, Daniel's body was found last night in his village of Santa Eulalia.

Daniel Pedro Mateo was a painter, teacher, a founder of Radio Snuq Jolom Konob, and a leader in the community resistance to mining and hydroelectric activities in Huehuetenango. Childhood experiences that exposed him to the grave inequalities and injustices confronting poor and indigenous communities in Guatemala motivated his lifelong commitment to work for a more just and humane society. After the armed conflict ended, he joined with other Qanjob'al Maya leaders in Santa Eulalia to start a radio station that would give voice to their community. They formed the majority of the local population, but they were nonetheless marginalized and silenced. Daniel was no longer involved in the day-to-day work of the station, but he maintained close ties with many of the current volunteer staff and leadership.

Many in the community believe this violent act to be a repercussion of Daniel's environmental activism. Lorenzo Fransisco Mateo, Daniel's cousin and fellow member of Radio Snuq Jolom Konob stated, "The only crime he was ever guilty of was fighting in defense of the environment". Daniel was an outspoken organizer against the Hydro Santa Cruz dam in Santa Cruz Barillas, a dam in his town of Santa Eulalia. A logging company, Maderas San Luis, had forced evictions of local Indigenous peoples. He was a member of Cultural Survival's partner organization, Asamblea de Pueblos de Huehuetenango, and member of the political party WINAQ, founded by Nobel prizewinner Rigoberta Menchu.

Daniel's death comes among a series of recent murders in Guatemala of Indigenous activists. Just last year, anti-dam activist and community leader, Andres Francisco Miguel, was shot and killed by security guards of Hydro Santa Cruz in Barillas, where Daniel was headed to host a workshop.

In March, Exaltación Marcos Ucelo, an Indigenous Xinca leader active against Canadian Tahoe Resources' silver mine in Jalapa was found beaten to death, after being abducted alongside three other Xinca leaders. Six months ago, seven Indigenous protestors were shot and killed by Guatemalan military in Totonicapan. These events reflect the dangerous state that Indigenous leaders and environmental activists find themselves in Guatemala.

Cultural Survival deplores these acts of violence, which are targeted specifically at Indigenous activists defending their rights and their lands. We extend our deepest condolences to the Mateo family and the people of Santa Eulalia. We call on the immediate investigation of this crime and an end to the persecution of Indigenous leaders. Community organizations in Santa Eulalia are calling for contributions to cover funeral expenses and to support Daniel's family in this difficult time. He leaves behind an ailing wife and eight children.

"I heard he was missing through BTS but I hoped it would be a better ending," Jeremias says. "He was kidnapped and tortured. They tried to cover this up, but they cannot, and it is wrong. This is 2013 and it is still happening."

I know he is thinking about his own experience with kidnappers. That horror, the torture, has been triggered by his friend's death, and I struggle to help bring him to a safer place.

"Let's take a break," I suggest as his voice trails off.

His head is bowed as his grip tightens on the bottle of apple juice he has been sipping. When he looks at me, I see a wall of tears banked against his soft brown eyes.

"Sometimes I feel like giving up," he whispers.

"But you won't," I reply.

"No. I won't," he says with determination. "More reason now than ever to tell the story." A spark has replaced the tears. "It is time to tell the true story of Guatemala."

21

Medicating the Demons and Looking for Help

For Jeremias, drinking alcohol became a way to medicate the pain. It had been a bad habit for many family members and friends, particularly his father, for a very long time. It was the answer to any kind of sadness, upset or anger. There was always a reason to have a drink for those who had no other way to deal with overpowering emotions, and even though he did not start as young as many others, Jeremias soon took up this family tradition as well. He recalls how happy his girlfriend, who would later become his wife, was that he did not drink like many others. He had never even tried alcohol. But that changed two years after he was married.

"My first drink was at the age of 24," he explains. "At the time, I did not get why all my local and international friends and colleagues wanted to drink. Many of them were making fun of me because I had not even had a sip of alcohol, but one day coming back from work that had been very traumatic for all of us, when my colleagues encouraged me to have a beer to cheer up, I said *yes*. I was so sad, tired, and frustrated so I took a beer and drank it. Then somebody else gave me another one, and then two more and soon I felt nothing. I was intoxicated and it was better than feeling all the other feelings I carried around and stuffed inside of me. But the next day, I was not prepared for the hangover. Oh, my goodness, I felt so bad. My head was pounding, and I could barely eat the soup we had for breakfast. I did not feel like it, but I had to continue with my work. I still did my work. It was definitely a bad experience, and I did not want to have another one like that. But I soon did.

"It was two or three weeks before I tried it again. I was with my colleagues in the home where many of them lived. My second experience was more in control. I drank what I thought would allow me to still be in control. The experience was different, but it was still too much drinking. In the beginning, I drank beers, but after a couple of months, I started to drink whiskey, rum, and the local liquor—anything, really. I usually drank only on the weekends, and I never missed one day of work from my drinking problem, no matter how sick I felt. But, even worse, because of my work role, I had a car and I drove several times under the influence of alcohol. I don't know how I drove. Often, I remembered nothing, and the next day when I woke up, I felt really scared. The first question in my mind was where or what happened to the car? I was always relieved when my wife would tell me it was in the garage. I cried so many times. I did promise several times. I did say *never again*, but it did not work. It just got worse, and these experiences kept happening again, again and again."

At this point in his life, Jeremias had never heard about PTSD, or how it might relate to his experiences or the way he faced his everyday reality. It was only after he came to Canada that he even learned he was considered a victim. From his point of view, his life was normal in a culture of violence.

"Many of us were like walking dead people," he says. "And certainly, my addiction to alcohol was my way to escape from my fears, my madness, my frustration. Most of the time I felt no fear, or I chose not to. We did not allow ourselves to cry, so it was frightening for me when I was drinking, and I would cry. I didn't know why, but it seemed like all the atrocities that we were victims from were sort of normal. So many of us went through it, and we were afraid to talk about it. We trusted no one and we were prohibited from talking about it. Even my parents never spoke of what happened to them or what they saw. We feared for our safety, so we chose to not talk about our fear and pains. And that is just too much silence!

"Since I was a little kid, I remember my father drinking a lot. At the beginning, it was so sad to see him passed out. He cried when he drank also, and when he was crying, I cried with him, even though I did not understand why. When he was happy, I was happy too. It was always obvious that the next day he did not remember what happened the day before. So, when I grew up, as a teen I got really upset and did not want him to be drunk. Several times I had to take care of him, and it wasn't pleasant. After these bad experiences with my dad, I did not want to become an alcoholic, and I told my mother that I would never do that. That is why I never started drinking earlier. But after a while, like my father, I had no other way to make it all go away.

"From the beginning, I don't think anyone around me was happy with my alcohol addiction. It was definitely not pleasant to be with an alcoholic, and it was a big problem for sure dealing with someone who wouldn't listen, and I often became aggressive and selfish. I have no idea how my wife handled me back then. In the beginning, she was the most caring person who always protected me. From my point of view, I had the full support of my wife, but one day when we were still in Guatemala she left me, because she suspected that as well as my drinking problem I also had other women as girlfriends. When I drank, I had no good judgment.

"At this time, we had just had our first son and she took him with her. This experience of losing my one and only child was certainly a really painful one, but even then, instead of going and asking my wife for forgiveness and apologizing for my actions, I kept working in the day time, and at night drinking and drinking again. Finally, one day on a weekend she came back, and oh my God, it was one of the most painful and memorable times for me, as my son is one of the most wonderful gifts that I have in my life. Once again, I talked with my wife and I made promises to stop drinking, so I could take care of them both. But they were not promises I intended to keep, because in my messed-up mind she was making fun of me.

"I could only think about what she had done wrong, and some of the things I knew about her interest in someone else in the past. I never saw my faults. I thought she had violated our marriage; she had hurt me by taking my son away from me. That is what I was really thinking, so my addiction became even worse. By now I felt I needed to have a drink for any excuse—happiness, anger, frustration, sadness, fear. It is obvious that my wife was the one most affected by my addictions and actions. I was not a good person to live with, and many times when she wanted me to stop drinking, I just didn't care, and when she was persistent, I hit her or pushed her away. She was always crying and was sometimes afraid of my anger. Many times, I didn't remember anything, but got to hear about it the next day.

"Even after all that, my wife was always a caring woman, who just wanted love and peace from her husband, the father of her son. But I was so mixed up, I could not give her what she needed. She always said, 'Take care of yourself, we love you,' but I know today I did not love myself, so how could I really love anyone else? There was too much drinking all the time now. When I was traveling from my work and got back from a long trip, I always planned to cook and invite all my relatives and friends to come eat and drink. It would start out as a happy gathering with food and music, but it usually ended in a miserable fight with my siblings, my parents, or my brothers-in-law. We spent a lot of time drinking together, too much drinking. Strangely, my mother-in-law defended me, even though I was destroying myself and hurting everyone around me.

"My habit of drinking never stopped until I came to Canada, but even then, it did not last. When I learned where to find alcohol I started to drink again, again, and again. A couple of times, I ended up sleeping in the street and taking a cab very early the next day. This even happened a couple of times in winter. Taxi drivers would take me home when I was too drunk. Once a taxi driver even took me to the wrong place, and I had to walk and got lost. Twice the city police incarcerated me for a night and the next day, after I was sober, they woke me up and told me it was time to go home. Sometimes, they drove me home and I am so thankful for their kindness, because otherwise I don't know what would have happened to me. I might have frozen to death.

"One night, I was so aggressive and wanted to go out and keep drinking, but my wife didn't want me to go. I was so intoxicated she ended up calling a friend and took our three children to sleep over at our friend's house. Another day, same situation, she decided to call my work director. That is when my addiction problem became much more obvious. My director spoke to me about all the negatives consequences of being an alcoholic, like losing my family and my job, and maybe even ending up dead. She suggested I look for help, so I decided to go to a mental health counsellor. I also called Addiction Services, and they suggested I attend the 12-Step meetings of Alcoholics Anonymous (AA). I knew I needed help, so I even approached and spoke to two counsellors from the John Howard Society."

Slowly, the seriousness of his situation started to dawn on Jeremias. Waking up at the police station or outside in wintertime, and not being able to be there for those he loved during times of need or crisis, made him realize he needed to make a change. He was estranged from his wife, who was now gone most of the time. He had used alcohol to cope when he heard of his mother's passing. This meant he was not able to help the rest of the family through this. He knew someone needed to take care of his children and his house. He needed to work, and he wanted to do his job well. It was a turning point.

"I was so sad and upset," he says. "By going and attending AA, I had to also hear the horrible tragedies of so many people as a consequence of their drinking habit, so I decided it was time for me too to stop drinking. I wanted to give my children a loving father. I wanted them to know, no matter what, I'm here for them. I left my home country to give them the best, a better life, and now I was very close to losing my wife and my children. No matter what else I'd been through, I knew I could not stand that."

It was the winter of 2011 when Jeremias made the decision to address his addiction and face the issues that caused him to need alcohol to cope. He was trying to move ahead with his life. He had just purchased the house where he still lives today and he felt some sense of accomplishment, but he still battled with the memories almost every day. He felt like his life was slipping away. He was tired and sad, and he wanted to change. He was becoming someone he didn't like or respect, and he knew that was not who he was really born to be. Unfortunately, his experience in trying to find help in the mental health field was not so successful. AA was a life-changing therapy for Jeremias, but his visits to a psychologist and a psychiatrist almost made him want to drink again. He shakes his head as he recounts the visits:

"I asked for help, but no one helped me there. The few times I went for counselling was not a good experience. I was nervous and afraid to trust, but I really wanted someone to talk to who could teach me ways to have a normal life. It seemed like all they wanted to do was give me prescriptions, or they just kept checking their watch to see if our time was up. This only made me trust even less. And they wanted me to talk about my past when I didn't even trust them enough to talk about today.

With all the prescriptions, I threw everything but the sleeping pills in the garbage. They gave me papers to read and asked some questions, but I wanted some tips to learn how to stay alive. I didn't even understand the language that well. How was I supposed to read their pamphlets? Sometimes I would try to open up by talking about something not so important, or just sitting quiet to get the strength, but it seemed like the counsellor could only see the clock, and ask me questions I could not even understand.

"I don't think it was hard to tell I felt sad. I couldn't understand why the counsellor asked me so much about what I was feeling. I think we both knew I was not there because I was happy. I wanted him to tell me what was wrong, and if there was a way for me to feel better. When I am told I have only 50 minutes to tell my story to a stranger I am not sure I can trust, I feel even more sadness. Sitting in the small room that reminded me of a police interrogation room only made me wish we could just go for a walk outdoors. Maybe there I could talk without fear."

Jeremias did not get the mental health help he was looking for, and he soon came to see that suitable mental health aid for refugees was non-existent. He tried his best to understand self-help books and articles, but he knew he needed more. He prayed to meet someone who would understand.

22

Spiritual Connection

AA talked about *spiritual awakenings* and *higher power* but did not dictate what that needed to look like, so Jeremias felt more at home with this 12-Step program. Spirituality was always important to him.

He explains: "Our Mayan faith practices are based on our belief that we are creatures who are all part of mother earth. We have a connection and are related to all. As an example, when we pray, we call on and connect with all. We try to always be in harmony with the trees, rocks, rivers, sky, with our ancestors; we call all human nature brothers and sisters, and we are never alone. It is my belief and understanding that we are here to take care of each other, of everyone, because you are me, and I am you. It is obvious that if you are me, you are not going to hurt me. That is how it should work.

"Also, in my faith we should have no fear, especially no fear of death. That is why when I was tortured many times, I never gave up. When I heard that I would be killed, with the firearm in my mouth or on my forehead that is why I replied, 'Just do it.' Somehow, I did not feel afraid; I was sure that I wasn't alone, since the 1980's when I witnessed the torture and genocide in life. My parents always taught us how we are protected by our ancestors, and that it is always important to be in communication with all gods—the God: heart of the sky, heart of Mother Earth, and the spirits of Mother Nature. I think my belief in the connectedness of all living things, that you are really me and I am really you, and that all is eternal—I think this definitely played a part in my survival. My faith in this miracle, that tells me I will never really die and that my ancestors stand with me, helped me get through.

"There are a lot of things that happened to me that I still don't understand. I know spiritual powers helped and protected me and my family. I still don't know how or why, when the military were torturing and burning our people and community, they did not notice us. Somehow, we were able to see them, but they did not see us. I think maybe it was a miracle of protection. Perhaps we were converted to a rock, a tree, a bird or simply air. I don't know! The only thing I remember is that when we witnessed these atrocities we were crying, yet it seems that nobody noticed us. Sometimes, the question for me is: was this a dream or was it real? I know it happened, I was part of it, but God's divine spirit somehow made a way for me to survive. When my grandmother warned me that Inup would make anyone near her at night disappear, I wonder if that is what she meant. When Inup hid us, did she really make us invisible like the legend says?"

Jeremias says that many times on his journey, he felt he was receiving supernatural help to get away from a bad situation. He goes on to explain: "Certainly whatever we want to call it—divine protection, miracle, *Higher Power*—one thing I always did even when I was segregated from the rest of my family, I never forgot to pray. It might seem like I was alone, but I believed my mom, dad, and all my ancestors were protecting me. I never ever forgot to pray. Escaping without shoes and my glasses from my kidnappers, who had guns that could have shot me easily from a distance—that was a miracle! No one saw me. I was running and my feet seemed to be flying away. To this day, I know I had some kind of divine help that day. Also, driving in a blackout and making it safely to a destination, I know God or the spirits must have taken care of me, too, because He knew I did not want to be that way."

Taking care of his spirit is still of utmost importance for Jeremias today, and he admits he still has struggles with alcoholism. He respects all faiths and will visit churches, but he finds his sanctuary mostly outside in nature. He says he knows God is there.

"Divine faith, God's gift, God among us, regardless of what your beliefs are, spiritually speaking, you will never be alone," he says. "Always, when you look deeply for guidance, you will find a way. When we feel sad, happy, or confused, we should continue to celebrate life, and even when we are in a challenging situation, if we have faith everything will in time go away. Perhaps we do not know if this scene in our life has purpose, whether it seems negative or positive, for our greater good, or to teach us. We should all understand and consider and bless any scene in life that we have."

Jeremias believes, as a Mayan man, that he was created for a purpose. That means any situation he goes through is part of a plan from the one who created him. It is his job to try to understand the lessons and ask for divine help, so he can learn what is needed to complete the tasks he was assigned before his birth. For this reason, he says asking 'Why?' and listening for answers can help guide him to what he needs to do. Even the pain brings its own lesson and can increase our faith.

He explains: "Miracles can happen only if you believe in them. All human beings are a small piece of an entire creation, a huge puzzle made by the creator, and it doesn't matter how small we are, we are still very important parts of the whole because there is a purpose for all of us. We are not just a casualty. We are creatures given a role to carry out, one that is important to this entire creation."

Jeremias says he still practices Christianity and what he learned from his Catholic religion. He has visited many other churches and says he knows God is there, wherever he goes. The traditions may differ, but the purpose is the same—to give thanks to God—and he does not see this as incompatible with his Mayan beliefs. For him it works, and it has often been the lifeline he needed, when he felt he could no longer go on in his own strength. Jeremias still often prays for help. He asks continually for direction to find purpose and strength in his quest to exorcise the memories that still cry out for attention—memories so painful that even self-medication barely soothes. He remains committed to helping all who need his help, but he is aware he still needs help too.

"I knew for a long time I needed to find someone I could trust, so I could tell my story," he says. "I prayed for that to happen, so I could start to heal."

Then our paths crossed. We met in the early spring of 2012. I was at the Multicultural Association of Fredericton meeting to talk about my work in therapeutic writing, and how I believe it can help survivors of trauma. I had already had meetings with settlement coordinator Ljiljana Kalaba to talk about the possibility of running a small 'life writing' group, that could provide an outlet for those who needed to tell their stories, and also help newcomers learn better English. That evening was my opportunity to give information to the group of almost 40 people, to see if anyone might be interested.

I sat in a seat near the back so I could look around and get a feel for the crowd in attendance. A few minutes before the meeting, a man who appeared to be of aboriginal ancestry slipped quietly into the seat beside me. He didn't speak but smiled when he turned to look in my direction. I smiled back and admired his long brown hair tied back in a ponytail. It was almost as long as mine, I thought to myself.

I shared briefly with the group about how writing my own story, with a co-author for support, had helped me heal from some of the sad things that had happened in my life. It was later published as *Little White Squaw: a white woman's story of abuse, addiction, and reconciliation*. I encouraged anyone who might be interested in telling their stories, or just learning a little bit more about writing in the English language, to come try out our group. After I spoke, Jeremias approached me and introduced himself. He was the man with the long ponytail who had been sitting beside me.

"I want to be in your group," he said. "And I would like to talk to you about the youth I work with in the schools. Maybe this can help them too."

The *River Writers* group started a couple of weeks later. The name was chosen by the nine men and women in attendance. They agreed that a river symbolized their connection, even though they came from several different countries, cultures, and backgrounds. To say I had taken on something much bigger than I expected was an understatement. The event was advertised as a "Creative Story Writing Meeting," and the first one was held on Wednesday, May 9, 2012. Jeremias was there in attendance, along with both male and female participants from Nepal, Sierra Leon, South Korea, Iran, Australia, Columbia, and Canada. These 'newcomers' had been in Canada long enough to be able to learn English, and they were eager to improve their writing skills, so they did not hesitate to participate in the first exercise: "Tell me your name and what it means to you?"

This exercise was intended to be a short icebreaker to help me get familiar with the individuals in the group. I had no idea it would be such a foundational piece in the story of each one there. They spoke proudly and sometimes with great emotion, and it filled up most of our time together that first evening. My 'agenda' was quickly rewritten as I developed on the spot the next exercise that naturally evolved from their stories. It left me feeling so humbled that they would trust me enough to share such an important part of their lives.

We met for a few weeks, but it quickly became apparent that my original plan to encourage therapeutic storytelling was not realistic, or in their best interests. Here were people from several different countries with their own customs and beliefs as well as their own histories, and we had both men and women in this group. This was not the setting to encourage personal or painful accounts of anyone's story, so we turned it into a creative writing group that employed safer questions about personal experiences or cultures. In the end, everyone seemed pleased with the experience, and two participants told me they wanted to tell their own story, to have it in a book. The young man from Sierra Leone who had been a child soldier said he might need my assis-tance in the future. Jeremias asked if I would be willing to write his, starting immediately. He said he was ready *now*.

This is what he has to say about this time: "I felt lost for so long! After going to different mental health professionals, I felt that there was no way to open up the doors of the truth and all the wounds with it, when I have such problems with trust. But when I heard Eve Mills Nash presenting about her work, I felt some hope. I decided I might try this way of therapy. I knew it would be a painful experience, but I also knew that if I kept myself in silence it would still hurt, and I would be contributing to the injustice that is happening right now against humanity.

"I was ready, and I was thirsty for support. When I heard her telling her story and she talked about writing the story into a book, I knew right away that was what I needed to do, so I joined the group. I felt hopeful. I knew I was a victim of a dirty war, and I wanted to share my story with society. I wanted to show that from our pain we can still live and be the change we want to see in the world. A world with a lot of hate, with a lot of violence, with gender discrimination, and oppression. I wanted to share the message that anger and sadness can revert to something beautiful. I was sure this was the only way that I could really teach my children to be at peace, even though we had had a rough time in life.

"I struggled too much. I tried several times to talk, but I couldn't. I think by telling my story, I want other survivors to feel that it is okay to be upset, it is okay to be angry, to cry, to feel alone, to share your pain. The hardest thing is the trust. I needed someone who could be patient and understand that sometimes I just can't talk. It is extremely hard to see myself as a little child being exposed to events that I shouldn't have been exposed to. They stole my childhood. The horror killed my way of being a human being. Several times, I had to pinch myself to make sure I was really alive. Too many times I tried to give up and just kill myself. To trust someone is so hard, but I knew I must if I am to live and tell this.

"This writer, Eve, was also a mental health therapist and she knew about suffering. She seemed to care and not just have an agenda, so I decided I might be able to trust her. But even then, there were times it was not easy. The hardest part of telling my story was always when I had to go back to talk about *little me*. I cannot accept how the system mistreated my community, my relatives being tortured and killed. It is so hard to go back and touch the wound.

"But when I think about what it did to innocent children, children like me and especially me, I am afraid and feel alone.

Telling this makes me extremely sad. I'm crying. This is not fair, but I have to do it. It must be told, but I could never have told this story alone. Only with the support of a professional who cares and tries to understand could I do this. Not only did I need her expertise as the writer and mental health professional, but I also needed her guidance and courage to work with me and really listen and allow me to lead. It has still not been easy, but at least it helps.

"I know this has not been easy for the writer either. It is hard to listen to this pain, I think, and not get affected. I know she was crying with me sometimes when I told my story. And I know there were times she waited for a long time to continue with me, sometimes months, because I just could not do it. It is hard to find just the right time or place to talk but, thank God, she never once looked at a clock while we were together. Sometimes, we met in a coffee shop, but the harder parts we did in her home or mine, or sometimes outside. We did not put time limits on it most of the time, and that helped because sometimes I could talk more than two hours, and other times only a few minutes. The story took its own time."

23

Peso: A Gift from a Mam Grandmother

The snow swirled spitefully in front of my labouring car as I turned into the recently plowed parking lot on the Exhibition Grounds in downtown Fredericton. It was December 26, 2013—Boxing Day. The electricity had been out at my home for three days due to a crippling ice storm that hit the east coast.

I was staying at the Delta hotel nearby. Christmas Eve and part of Christmas Day at my daughter's home in Noonan had not been our usual festive holiday gathering. The storm, serious illness, and family discord overshadowed any attempts to celebrate. Even the golden-brown turkey and all the eye-catching accessories did little to whet my appetite as I digested the latest news of my middle daughter's prognosis—brain damage that might be signaling something even more deadly. I checked into the hotel mid-afternoon, along with my eldest daughter, Heather, craving the sleep that would give my mind a break from the cares of the week. For a few hours I was given a reprieve as I settled under the thick white comforter and Heather watched TV. When I woke this morning it all came crashing back, so I decided I would make my day a productive one; I needed a distraction.

As I stepped from the car, I felt a cold chill grip my body as the icy wind assaulted my bare cheeks. I was sad, but I looked forward to this meeting. I figured it would be much more productive to meet with Jeremias and work on his story, rather than focus on my own woes. He was already inside the Tim Horton's coffee shop. I saw him seated at a corner table as soon as I entered. He was still wearing a thick brown winter hat with ear tabs pulled down over his ears as he busily texted on his phone.

"It must be hard for him to tolerate this weather," I thought to myself. *"I bet he really misses Guatemala on days like this."*

"Nice day," I said as I approached with my hot ginger latte in hand.

He rose, smiled, and gave me a welcoming hug.

"I love it!" he said with a boyish grin. "Sure you do!" I replied with a chuckle. "You crack me up."

It had been my intention to spend the next hour or so asking more detailed questions about Jeremias' life, but he turned the tables on me.

"How come you look so sad?" he asked.

"I'm fine," I answered with a smile.

"No, you're not," he said. "What's wrong?"

I explained a few things, bringing him up to date on my somber Christmas, and my frustration that I could not change what was happening in my family or my daughter's health.

"You need to stop taking care of everyone else," he said to me. "You are not everyone's mother and you don't have to take on that role, even with your kids, twenty-four hours per day. Your children are grown."

"I know," was all I could manage, hoping to change the subject, but he continued.

"A new year is starting, so you should use your strength for yourself; then help everyone else. You are wearing out. You don't look happy these days."

"I try to look after myself," I started to explain.

"But you don't, and you have to. Every day you are alive has a purpose and every day you are alive is a happy day. Our people have nothing, but we are happy people. Sometimes you just have to choose the joy."

"Wow!", I thought to myself. I've just been reminded of what I'd often told my own clients, family, and friends. Somehow, I'd forgotten to tell *me*. What a reality check, a special gift, to hear Jeremias after all the challenges he's faced remind me there is never a reason to stay sad. That's when he reached inside his wallet and handed me the peso.

"A gift," he said, "now, for you."

Then he told me the story of its journey: Jeremias had worked in the Campeche and Quintana Roo refugee camps. It was August 1995, in one of these refugee camps in Mexico, that he met someone he would later come to think of as an earth angel. The woman looked tired, but there was a light in her face that drew Jeremias, even though she had not yet spoken a word to him. In this camp, where many now dressed like those in this new country, she beckoned to him without words as she sat quietly in her traditional Mayan dress.

Jeremias was there at the refugee camp to talk to leaders in the community who wanted to return to their homeland in Guatemala. It was one of his monthly visits to provide support on behalf of his organization, funded by the United Nations Refugee Agency, an organization that played a large role in the negotiation of the repatriation and return of refugee families from Mexico, which resulted from the conversation and peace agreement between the Guatemalan government and the guerrillas. Repatriation was for the people who wanted to go back. Some had already accepted land and citizenship from Mexico, but most of the people still longed for home. These were the people he tried to help.

"Hello. How are things?" Jeremias asked the elderly woman in Spanish.

"What do you mean?" she returned. "You know how things are. You know what happened to us."

"I mean, how are you feeling in this strange land?" He felt an instant kinship when she replied, "I have to go back."

When she began to tell him part of her story, Jeremias felt himself carried back in time with her.

She was a *Mam* grandmother. *Mam* is a Mayan language spoken in Huehuetenango, Guatemala. Many of the Mam population had to immigrate to Ixcan, Quiche, before civil war began, and by the end of the 1970s and beginning of the 1980s, all the Mayan communities who resettled in Ixcan, Quiche, had to go and look for refuge in neighbouring Mexico. This grandmother had been in the refugee camp for 15 years. She began to talk about El peso, our Mayan calendar, the times, the circle of life—words Jeremias would never forget.

"Son, I want to give you this peso because it has a lot of meaning for me," she told him. "To some people it might not be special, but for me, when I came here with nothing, it was the first strange money that I ever saw, different from our normal one. It was difficult for me to get familiar with it at first, but then I saw it had a special purpose and meaning. I saw our Mayan calendar, the circle of life, in it and I came to see it had power for me and my family.

"This money has some power because it has been with me all the time from when I got it until now, and I have been praying with it. Son, if you believe it can be your protector, so please do me a favor, take this as a gift from me."

Jeremias did not want to take the peso away from the grandmother, but she insisted. He felt a strong connection as she placed it in his hands and continued to speak:

"When you feel like something doesn't make sense, when you are upset or sad, when you think you are at risk—you know, son, my belief is it has been helping me and my entire family forever, and it will help you. I see you as a good helper to many people; you do a lot. You never told me, but I know."

The grandmother's dark eyes seemed to look into his heart as she continued: "You look very sad, but you have something very special. I want to tell you that you are not alone. Our creator is always with you; from the beginning of your journey and every day, someone powerful is taking care of you and your family. Please always remember that you have a lot to offer and you have been chosen to help."

Jeremias said he felt afraid as he continued to listen to her words:

"You will travel a lot to advocate for our people. You will be confused and have much frustration. You will cry and you will feel like you are in a dark room alone. You will even try to harm yourself, and one day someone will see you as bad and want to get rid of you. But for sure, you will be walking away as if nothing happened. You will be in a big place and you will talk differently. Last night I had a dream, and that's why I wanted to meet you and give you this coin, because for me it is a symbol of hope."

Even though her words did not make sense, he knew this was a very special gift, so he accepted it with gratitude.

"I wish you the best and if I meet you again, it will be in Guatemala," he said as he smiled and walked away.

Jeremias never saw the grandmother again. She told him her last name was *Sales*. He looked for her many times on future visits but could never find her. He began to wonder if he had dreamed it all, but then there was still the peso. It was real. Jeremias asked his Mayan father to pray over the peso and told him the story. Then he took the peso and added it to other sacred objects—rocks and earth from his village—that he kept on an altar in his home, where he said prayers daily. When he came to Canada, the peso and many of the other special treasures came with him, and he began to carry the peso in his wallet. Every time he looked at it, he wondered if the gift-giver had been a real woman or an angel.

"Many times, I held that peso and prayed for strength. It helped take away the negative thoughts when I concentrated on the words she said to me in that camp," Jeremias explains to me as we sip hot coffee oblivious to the world of ice and snow outside. "There were times I hurt myself, and times other people tried to hurt me, like she said. Even when I turned to alcohol to take away my pain, I was hurting myself. Four or five years ago, there were times I did not think I would make it. I thought about suicide, but today I do believe I was born for a purpose, just like you."

I wasn't sure what to say when Jeremias finished. I felt suddenly humbled and empowered at the same time. A fleeting question glanced across my mind. "*Are you my angel today, Jeremias?*" But I did not say the words out loud.

"Why me, Jeremias?" I asked. "Why would you give this to me?"

"Because you need it," he said. "You helped me trust enough to start telling my story, and that is opening a new chapter in my life. I am happy every day now. I believe there is protection and joy in this, and I want you to have it. Just to remember you have a purpose, and every day is a happy day."

"I don't know what to say," I told him.

"Don't say anything," he laughed. "Just tell me you will stop taking care of everyone else before yourself."

"I will, Jeremias," I told him "It will be my goal for 2014. That, and helping you tell your story."

"Then we share a good goal," he agreed as we continued to chat for the next hour about his second trip to Guatemala earlier that year. Little did either of us know on that day that it would take another five years to finish the story.

24

Back to Guatemala: Torn between Two Worlds

In March 2013, Jeremias received a phone call from his younger brother telling him his father was really sick. He was recovering from prostate surgery and was now battling an infection. He had been in a clinic for two procedures. Jeremias' sister, who was still a practicing physician, felt it was time he came to see his father, because no one was sure how much time he had left. Jeremias had mixed feelings. He was worried about his dad and wanted to see him, but he was also nervous about another trip back to the country that still held the threat of personal danger for him. In the end, the love for his father won out. Still, there was fear accompanying him as he set out on the light rom the Fredericton airport around 4 am on the day of his departure. His account of this trip displays the myriad emotions through which he traveled:

"When I left Fredericton, I was so sad because I was leaving my children behind," he says. "My heart was heavy because I did not know if I would find my ather alive. I worried about all the security protocol in Montreal Customs to cross into the USA. I always have these headaches when I travel to the USA. When I reached the Montreal airport, I was a little hesitant because of my first travel experiences to Guatemala, and the passport issues in the customs during previous flights. And sure enough, it looked like another troublesome flight. When I was crossing the line to board my next plane headed for Denver, I was stopped and sent to the customs office. My heart started beating faster. I elt nervous and confused, remembering past experiences, but this time it was different. This time the customs officer was very gentle. He asked if I had been having troubles before when I was traveling into the USA. I told him right away, 'Yes.'

"Since he was so kind, I asked him if he could please explain what was wrong with my passport, and why I have to be stopped all the time by a Customs Officer. He explained that I needed to fix my passport with all my first names and last names. The problem was that originally I had four names, and when I got my Canadian Citizenship, Citizenship and Immigration Canada recognized just three names, but did not include my fourth. He told me there was some individual who had the same last name as me who had been deported from the USA. After this explanation and the friendly way this gentleman explained it to me, I was relieved. It only took about 30 minutes, so I was on time for the next plane and was so excited, I bought a coffee and just relaxed and waited to board the plane."

The rest of the flight was uneventful for Jeremias. He spent the night in Denver before boarding the final flight to Guatemala City. He arrived around at 10 am the next day. Although he was nervous and trying not to think about the dangers that still lurked for him in his birth country, memories of some of those perilous times did their best to surface. In the end, he was able to push them away with the excitement of reuniting with his birth family.

"When I arrived in Guatemala airport, I was very confused because people were so polite and so kind offering help, even to use a cell phone if I needed it," he says. "But, since I did not know whether to trust them or not, I was still anxious. I did not see my sister anywhere, so I started to panic. I approached a taxi driver and asked if I could use his cell. I told him I needed to call my friend who was supposed to pick me up, but she was not there yet. But it was only a few minutes later that I saw them. My sister and her husband and their daughters were at the airport to pick me up.

"Oh my God! When she came close, we both started to cry. When I'd left Guatemala in 2002, Alba was still doing her post-secondary education, studying to be a doctor. Now she was married with two beautiful daughters. Our encounter brought back memories of a lot of pain, as well as some very beautiful ones. Mainly when I think about my little sister, I think about how I was always looking after her, and now what a big change. She didn't look like she needed me to look after her now! Everything was changed.

"After my arrival, they took me for lunch in a busy place with many people, a food court. I had to really think about what I would eat. With so much pollution I remembered in this city, I was afraid to get sick, so I got some Thai food; I thought that would be safe. I wanted to have coffee, so my brother-in-law went to get it at McDonalds. It was strange to even think about something you see so much in Canada being part of the place where I once lived. It had changed so much.

"Unfortunately, I got a stomachache as soon as I left. We figured out the pure milk used in the coffee was too much for me. It was not pleasant, and I began to get nervous. Everywhere there was different food, everything was new for me, not what I remembered. I was scared when I saw people with weapons, carrying pistols. They were civilians with no private security uniforms. My first impression was that these people were killers. I did not hesitate to point this out and tell my sister and she replied: 'No worries, just act normal.'

"As we travelled in their Mazda I looked around. I thought, *'this is not Guatemala.'* I was shocked; the population seemed to have tripled. There were so many more people and cars, barely space to walk, and hardly a tree anywhere. It never used to be like that. It seemed like I was in another world. There was even a parking garage. There had never been a need for this when I lived in Guatemala. We were on the way to the clinic. They had just operated on my dad the night before. It was about 45 minutes from Santiago Sacatepequez.

"When I first saw my dad, I thought how much he had changed since 2009. I could not believe how old and helpless he looked. I started to cry. I spent all night at the clinic taking care of my father. It was definitely a long night. I was praying; I did not want my dad to go yet. I felt a lot of frustration and deep sadness. I was talking to my father; even though he did not answer, I never gave up talking to him. I would hold his hand. I told him how angry I felt, how I loved him and hated him at the same time.

"The second day, my sister took me to her home to get some sleep. When we got there, I had to pass through security to go to where she lives. I was surprised. They asked: 'Who are you?' They wanted my ID. I was nervous, but it was a beautiful neighbourhood, so I started to relax. This was a place where people have money, not poverty. I was surprised to see everyone had a car. There were not even many buses around when I lived there.

I went back that night to take care of my dad once again. It was a very blessed night for me. Sometime between my talking to this still man on the bed and my tears, I heard someone saying, 'Why are you crying? Who are you?' Immediately, I jumped up and hugged him and gave him a kiss on his forehead, and I told him that I was his son. At first, he didn't believe it. He couldn't see. He said, 'No, my son is far, far away; he is in Canada.' I replied, 'Dad, it is me', and he immediately started to touch my head and my ponytail and began to talk. 'How are you? How are my grandchildren doing? Is everyone doing ok? Please take a good care of them.'

"It was amazing. We talked the entire night; we both really enjoyed our time together. We talked about being thankful he was a dad who wanted us to have an education and taught us that God loves us. He taught us we needed to contribute to society. I told him I forgave him for leaving, for making me responsible for my younger sister and brother—and I really did forgive him; the anger was gone. Now, I felt it had been my honour to do this. He had already told me many times how he understood my hate towards him for disappearing. I told him about how I had to beg sometimes just to get medicine for my siblings. I thanked him for helping to make me stronger. It turned out to be a gift. And after all I realized, *it was just one scene of my life!*

"He told me he prays for me a lot and for my children. He said he could now die in peace. I told him it was not time; he still had so much to share, to offer, from his encyclopedia on life. I wanted more time to learn about things from him. He had so much patience and overcame so much. He blamed himself for leaving us. I wanted him to know I understood why he had to do it, so he could be at peace. We talked a lot."

The next part of the visit held very special significance for Jeremias. He returned to what had been a large part of his childhood community—the one from which he fled as a child—and he visited his mother's grave. He was not brave enough to travel the extra distance to where his home had been destroyed by fire, and where he and his family had hidden in the arms of Inup.

When Jeremias speaks of this visit, he does so with great reverence and emotion:

"After taking care of my dad at the clinic, my brother-in-law and my sister took me to Rabinal BV. I was not able to be there when my mother passed away in November 2009, but now I would be able to give my love and respect to the place where she was buried. It was a wonderful trip and brought back a lot of memories. It took four hours in the car. Along the way, the roads were so much better than I could remember. Some places used to take so long because the roads were very bad. As we came to each community, I remembered how these places looked in the 70s.

"The memories also carried a kind of panic. As we travelled, I sometimes thought: *'What if it happens again? Could that car be coming for me?'* Suspicion was still there. I knew the way I was dressed, and my hair made me look different. Now, after living in Canada and having first learned Spanish and then English as my new first languages, I was aware I spoke Achi with an accent. When we entered Rabinal, I felt so much fear as I looked around. I saw the happiness of the children, so different from the terror of my youth there. It seemed strange to see all the cars and houses with two or three floors replacing the humble neighbourhoods I remembered. But what I recalled most was the bloodshed. It was hard to keep the pictures out of my head, but I fought to do it. I remembered the trees, the beautiful trees, especially Inup, the tree that saved my life and the lives of my mother and my siblings. The ones here were not as big as the one that had sheltered us, but I could still see it in my mind.

"It was a market day. I visited the church with my sister. Memories, both good and bad, threatened to swallow me up. It was so sad. I felt so confused. I love this land of my birth. I asked God why I had to be so far away from my home, but there was no answer for me. When we visited my mother in the cemetery ten minutes from the church, it was the first time since 2000 I had been in that cemetery. It had been upgraded. There was a wall that had not been there before. I thought it was quite fancy. They even had vaults. I was surprised. There were many candles. It was a happy place. I brought flowers we had bought in the market and candles, which we lit. I felt the peace, the connection, and the belonging immediately. I still keep candles with me everywhere, even at home today. It helps me remember

I always have light in my life. I really wanted to be there in 2009 for my mom when she passed, but I was too afraid. I wanted to see my mom, and that day I felt like she was right there. I told her I was sorry I didn't get there in 2009. I told her how much I loved her.

"We stayed for half an hour. Everyone was deep in silence, and we shared our respect for our mom. I felt connected and good. I felt like she was at peace and she was happy, like she could hear my words and that was special. I got the opportunity to visit two monuments of my brothers and sisters, who were victims of the genocide in Rabinal BV in the 70s and 80s. My mom's grave was close to these monuments, but at the monuments the feeling was totally different.

Something really strange happened to me after I visited my mother and connected with her. I smiled and cried; the closure for me was done in a meaningful way. But as soon I approached the monuments and the place where the hundreds and hundreds of victims (children, pregnant women, grandmothers and parents from Rio Negro) were buried or represented by name, I couldn't contain my tears and I cried for a long time. I felt the pain. I offered them candles and *pom*. (*Pom* is the main Maya incense, a resin used in Maya religious ceremonies). I started to read the names. My uncle, my dad's brother, was there, too. He had been placed there after the exhumation.

"The names of those who disappeared are also on a plaque in a church in Guatemala City, but there in Rabinal I could feel the pain so much more. The memories covered me, but I was still thankul to be there. That day was deinitely a blessing, even though it was also a really challenging one. I was so glad I was able to go there. We left Rabinal at approximately 4 pm and got to Guatemala City the same day. It was a quick trip, but well worth it, even though the emotions were churning inside me. I knew those spirits were not all at peace; I could still feel the pain. I felt cold and as if somehow, I was responsible. At times, the confusion was overwhelming, but I tried not to let my feelings show."

Leaving Guatemala was almost as hard for Jeremias as it had been to make the decision to visit. He was torn between the two worlds. His siblings did not want him to leave so soon. He had not told them exactly when he would be going. He felt the pull to stay, but it was stronger to leave.

"I wanted to leave because of my children, but I also wanted to spend more time with my sisters, my brother and my father," he says. "But for my safety I had to leave. This time I felt much better than my first trip. I had more chances to see and visit important places, but the fear was always present. I couldn't walk alone; I knew it was still just too dangerous for me. But I had more opportunity to enjoy my stay, and it left me missing what I'd left behind, and sometimes wondering where I really belong. It was a violation of my rights to lose this feeling of belonging and of trust; I do not trust. I see that in Guatemala there is a huge change, but there is still poverty and danger. It brought back a lot of memories to go there, to be with my dad and my family, to visit Rabinal and talk to my mom; I felt the positive happiness, and also black memories."

Monument for Victims of Genocide in the Town of Rabinal Cemetery

Painting on one of the Monuments

The monument was erected in memory of those who were massacred or disappeared, most especially 77 women and 100 children, in Rio Negro, Rabinal

The flights back to Canada were uneventful for Jeremias. The privilege of having a Canadian passport when returning to Canada eliminated the long line-up with the international travelers, where suspicious security searched for any sign of non-compliance with regulations and laws. Jeremias was greeted in a small line-up of North American citizens and passed without incident. But the inner turmoil that he battled after his visit to Rabinal was less friendly and persisted throughout the flights home. His heart was again heavy and torn between the two worlds. Arriving in Fredericton, he carried the conflict with him.

He explains: "I was really happy to see my children and I felt so connected to them, but something else was still pulling at my heart. I asked myself: *'What am I doing? Where do I belong?'* My children needed me, and I knew I had a responsibility to care for them. But didn't my people need me too? 'Is there more I am supposed to do?,' I wondered. For the next four weeks I did my best to be there for my children, but emotionally speaking I was torn between the two worlds."

For more than a month after his return to Canada, Jeremias wrestled with his emotions and thoughts. Even his dreams gave him little peace.

"I felt both connected and disconnected with my spirit," he says. "Sometimes I felt I belonged back in Guatemala. It had been so sad to reconnect to that part of my reality, my past, and still have to get to know another part of me, the part of me who lived safely in Canada, but who was still controlled in my thoughts by this culture of danger and death, of being at risk.

Maybe in Canada I did not think so much about this background of violence and death, because in this new country I was in a new culture, the culture of running freely and taking care of myself, being without fear. I could think about good health instead of just staying alive.

"Visiting Guatemala triggered many things in me, but it also made me realize and appreciate the peace and freedom where I live now. As much as I longed for the home I remembered be-fore the time of death and destruction, I know I'm blessed to live in this context of peace in my new home in Canada. So many others never got this chance."

25

A Small Bit of Justice

Is this just the beginning of a story, a story of justice?

These words come to me from Jeremias in an email on Monday, May 13, 2013, along with the following account from the Breaking the Silence network:

Friends, I write today as history is made. Justice, at last, will be served in Guatemala! Today, in a packed courtroom, Judge Yassmin Barrios and the tribunal which accompanied her gave their verdict: Efrain Rios Montt, de facto military president from March 1982 to August 1983, guilty of genocide and crimes against humanity.

In her ruling, Judge Barrios declared, "There cannot be peace without justice in Guatemala."

She reiterated that genocide has affected all Guatemalans. and urged the public prosecutor's office to investigate and indict others responsible for genocide. Barrios began by noting that genocide did occur in the Ixil region of the Department of Quiche in 1982. Its purpose was to wipe out clandestine groups which the military branded as the support base for the guerrilla. The military government of the time, and its head of state, Efrain Rios Montt, saw the Ixil population as rebels to be destroyed. They used a scorched earth policy to decimate communities and used physical and psychological violence. Hunger was also a tool, and crops were burnt down over and over again, and people were forced to live in the mountains in fear. Men were forced to join the Civil Defense patrols. People lived with ongoing extreme stress, forced to live in model villages under constant control.

Barrios repeated that the indigenous Maya Ixil were systematically and repeatedly massacred, and that indiscriminate patterns of violence were shown. She emphasized that women were used as objects of war, and that rape and sexual violence against women, girls and the elderly were used to destroy the Ixil culture and dehumanize the population. Torture and rape were ways that the military tried to destroy the social fabric of the society. She also mentioned that the military tried to destroy the culture and cut the community's ties with their ancestors by destroying cultural and religious sites. The community wasn't able to continue its religious ceremonies and was prohibited from expressing its true identity.

Barrios reiterated that in all, 5.5% of the Maya Ixil population was destroyed in less than two years, and they have waited over 30 years for justice. She also mentioned that children were left affected, indeed that generations of Guatemalans have been scarred. They were left to believe that the indigenous race was inferior. Racism is at the root of genocide. Finally, Barrios reaffirmed that through the military plans presented, Rios Montt was in constant communication with the troops on the ground.

He gave and received messages at least every fifteen days, often more. The violence that was committed in the Ixil region wasn't spontaneous. The patterns, such as communities being burnt down, women raped, children captured, men tortured and killed, repeated themselves—an element of the doctrine of genocide. In the end, she said, there was no way that as head of state, Rios Montt was unaware of what was happening. In fact, she believes that he knew everything that was happening and did nothing to stop it.

"It's illogical to say that he didn't know what was happening," she said.

In the end, Rios Montt has been found guilty of genocide and crimes against humanity against the Maya Ixil people from March 1982 until August 1983, when he was de facto president. The maximum sentence for genocide is 30 years, but Barrios gave an additional 20 for the magnitude of the crime. He received an additional 30 years for crimes against humanity, totaling 80 years. Rodriguez Sanchez, ex de facto head of military intelligence, was absolved of all charges. The plaintiffs couldn't prove he was responsible for what was happening in the region.

Claudia Samayoa from the Unit for the Protection of Human Rights Defenders said: "Hopefully we will have a change in Guatemala and we will start to recognize that what is happening today, with the resistance against mining or explorations without due consultation, is part of the same idea of genocide. It is the same racism. It is the same idea that people are not worthy of decision-making. If we start to learn lessons from this trial, we will change as a country. There will no doubt be a swarm of legal challenges and appeals. But for tonight, many will finally sleep in peace.

"With appreciation for your solidarity! In honor of our grandchildren, girls, mothers, grandmothers, grandparents, brothers, and sisters, who suffered the impact of the genocide in Guatemala, Justice and Justice, Guatemala Never Again."

Jeremias felt many emotions when he heard this news. Initially he was happy to hear the verdict. This legal outcome was an important step forward for him and for his ancestors. The public acknowledgement of the suffering caused by Rios Montt, his army, and others like him, provided a small bit of justice for the horror suffered by so many innocent people.

But the ruling also brought back his memories and the sadness and anger with it. He found it hard to sleep and thought often about the slaughter of his people and his own escape as a child. He was also skeptical that this man would ever be brought to justice. It was no surprise to him when the conviction was later overturned by the constitutional court, which argued Rios Montt had been denied due process. For the next two years, the battle was fought in the courts with small minor victories, but none brought true justice for the crimes committed.

26

Full Circle

In May 2016, Jeremias returned to Guatemala for the third time. This time he felt less afraid about Customs, but he was still nervous about the trip. He knew he would face different fears when he travelled to Rabinal.

"The reason I was going to Guatemala was to be a part of a human rights delegation to visit our community partners there," he explains as he recalls the visit, sitting in my kitchen drinking strong coffee over our breakfast of quesadillas, corn bread and beans. He enjoyed the meal, I could tell, but I'm sure he'd have preferred to add a few jalapeños. He was excited about the trip. The community partners were primarily comprised of women's groups and other human rights workers. The aim was to include visits to the mining sites to see what was happening there. Jeremias was very aware of just how dangerous this could be. Already 12 political prisoners had been detained because they protested against mining, and people had been killed. The stories of the victims were common news in the communities, but often were not featured by the press.

Jeremias' head was swimming with conflicting feelings when he left from the Fredericton airport that spring morning on the flight to Toronto. He thought about the years that had passed since he last saw his village, and he knew he would not dare venture to where his home once stood. He would go to Rabinal, but La Ceiba was still out of bounds for him. It had been 18 years since he last saw the tree that had saved him. From Toronto, he flew directly to San Salvador, the capital of El Salvador. There, he boarded a plane to Guatemala where he would meet up with the rest of the delegation. Eventually, he would also see his father and sister. He was excited and happy, but also troubled.

"It had been so long since I visited that part of Rabinal and the other villages where I used to work, and I remembered so many things, good and bad, that had happened since then," he says. "I had always stayed in touch through BTS, but that is not the same as touching the ground where you once walked and where all the memories come to life."

Jeremias and the other BTS delegation members arrived in Guatemala City in time to celebrate May Day. May Day is also known as Labor Day in Guatemala and is a public holiday. It is associated with the start of spring as well as the celebration of workers and is celebrated with parties and parades. In 2016, it fell on May 1; in some years it falls on the day before or after. One of the BTS delegates described this part of her visit: "The streets were full of vibrant people participating in the march. The park was full, children were singing, and people were dancing. The energy in the air was beautiful and inspiring."

Jeremias couldn't help but recall how he had once marched on these same streets. He felt the excitement. On the second day, the group started by travelling to a mining community, where Goldcorp's Marlin Mine was (and still is today) devastating the land. They met with a women's organization who spoke passionately about the negative effects the Goldcorp mining Corporation has on their homes, their water, and their land. A tour by minibus showed the devastation up close. Jeremias learned more about the damages to the land and fertility of the mountain soil. He says it was shocking to see how houses have been cracked in two by the mining corporation, and what is taking place in terms of damage to the water supply.

According to a BTS delegate: "The comparison of the land and mountain range in this particular area as opposed to others that we have seen was quite dissimilar. The mine has turned the mountains into almost desert-like terrain, instead of the beautiful forests and crops that once grew on them. Instead of being able to produce their own crops, contamination has caused a need to resort to other means of providing for their families."

In addition, many of those who live near Goldcorp's Marlin Mine have experienced severely cracked homes since the mine began operating in 2005. And, even though the mine closed in 2017, the risks of the ongoing devastation will last for more than a century.

"This was so heartbreaking for me," Jeremias recalls. "It was painful to see just how much destruction is taking place, and how much of the land has been lost."

On day three, the BTS delegation met with members of the Huehuetenango Assembly (ADH). Delegate Sheena Cameron reported: *CEIBA and members of the Assembly of the Department of*

Huehuetanango (ADH) speak about their experiences defending their territory and life. They are organizing and mobilizing communities in the Department of Huehuetanango, and in other areas of Guatemala, for self-determination, and in resistance to the intrusion and violence perpetrated against them and their land by transnational corporations for mining and hydroelectric projects. The strength, courage and determination of these people continue to inspire me and demonstrate the power of a people united.

The unity of communities and people seems to be one of the biggest threats to neoliberalism and neocolonialism, which is why 'divide and conquer' tactics are yet again being employed by the Guatemalan government and transnational corporations. When communities are divided from within, it becomes easier for them to take advantage, to extract resources and manipulate individuals. We learned recently that the government is resurrecting the ex-civil patrols, which existed as a form of suppression within communities during the internal armed conflict, creating suspicion between neighbors. By threatening them with jail time, ex-civil patrols are influenced to intimidate members of ADH who are in defense of the land, to facilitate the projects of transnational corporations. Once again, we see that access to land and resources is at the heart of this struggle.

However, the community consultations that ADH has been organizing over the last ten years have seen approximately 500,000 people participate, and have served to reweave the social fabric of indigenous communities that was destroyed during the internal armed conflict, creating a reunification of communities. This participation and the self-determination of communities in the Huehuetanango area that members of ADH spoke about inspire great hope. They are redefining and reconstituting an understanding of development that reconnects people to Mother Earth and rejects an unsustainable way of life.

Key within this process has been the importance of relationships, within communities, with the land, and with those in solidarity with people defending their territory through international accompaniment, in which BTS plays a significant role. This reminds us of the interconnectedness of us all, and that we each have a role and responsibility to play to create unity for the ongoing struggle for justice.

The next day the delegation had a chance to listen to presentations at the Comite Campesino del Altiplano (CCDA) offices, and later went on a tour of the coffee bean processing plant and corn seed storing projects. In the evening, there was a Mayan ceremony. The CCDA originated in March 1982, in San Martín Jilotepeque, Chimaltenango, Guatemala, during the worst period of the Guatemalan Civil war. Its original name was The Peasant Committee for the Defense of the Highlands. Today, their coffee products can be found in many countries.

Time was also spent with the host families. Jeremias savoured every minute of this journey. But it was Monday, May 9, that he remembers most. Back in the days when Jeremias still worked in Guatemala, he had a dream that was just beginning to unfold. He and his fellow workers wanted to see a school established where the children could learn about their culture, and speak in their own language, a place where the truth could be known about the bloody history of the Achi people. This dream was to be the New Hope Foundation (FNE). The

New Hope Foundation in Rio Negro was created in 1997 by Jesús Tecú Osorio, who was a survivor of this violence.

Their official website describes the creation of the Foundation: *The greater municipality of Rabinal (population 40,000) was deeply affected by Guatemala's internal armed conflict. Most of its villages were burned to the ground, killing in the act women, men, grandparents, and children. All of them belonged to the Indigenous Maya Achi ethnicity. Throughout Guatemala, Indigenous communities like ours were accused of belonging to guerrilla movements, and even though it wasn't true the Guatemalan state ordered the army to carry out the massacres.*

The village of Río Negro was the site of one of the worst massacres in the war and has become iconic of massacres in Guatemala from that period. It was also where Jesús Tecú Osorio lost his parents and siblings. Due to his courageous struggle in exposing clandestine mass graves and bringing charges against the murderers of his family and his community in Guatemalan courts, he received the Reebok Human Rights Award, valued at 25,000 USD.

In January 1997, Jesús Tecú Osorio joined up with other survivors from Río Negro to form the board of directors of a new organization that was established to take advantage of the funds. They decided to call it the New Hope Foundation (FNE).

BTS was also part of this movement, and by 2016 more than 100 students were able to participate in the Guatemalan immersion experience in Rabinal, and witness first-hand how life can take on new meaning. The highlight for Jeremias was a visit to the school. The dream that was born after the massacre was now a reality.

"We knew it would start with having a chance to continue education," Jeremias explains. "We thought it would help not to forget the stories and be prepared for what could happen. In Guatemala, it is a privilege to stay in school. Most children only go until they are eight or nine years old, when they are strong enough to go and work for the family. We wanted a place (middle and high school) where education was still available to children after this age, a place where they would learn to be proud of their Achi culture."

Jeremias goes on to clarify that even though everyone knew the children needed to be educated in Achi, and hear the stories of what happened to their ancestors, everyone was afraid to talk about it or teach the history as it really happened. This changed, thanks to Jesús Tecú. Today, the stories are being told. There is even a museum in Rabinal with artifacts from the massacres, like the actual skull of an unknown victim; an AK47, and machetes used to kill people; rope that was tied around a victim found in one of the clandestine cemeteries, even necklaces worn by victims. The museum shows this part of the Mayan culture from the 1960s-1980s in a way that leaves no doubt about what happened.

Another one of the BTS delegates, Ida MacPherson, describes the day at the New Hope Foundation and Education Centre: *We were welcomed by Gloria, who is in her first year as Director of the New Hope Education Centre. In her presentation, we learned that the Centre is defined by their work in agriculture and the values of Mayan Achi culture. We learned that there are 80 students in the basic program of Grades 7-9, and 43 in the diversified program, which is for the older youth. (35% are female students).* She took us on a tour of the Education Centre: the infirmary where we met Sister Martha, who told us lots about the medicinal gardens; large gardens where the students were preparing to plant the corn; two female students told us about the amaranth crop that would soon be ready to harvest; and we toured the cattle and hens.

The school has expanded in the past years, and now includes dorms for the boys and girls who live so far away. They have dreams to expand to have programs to help the elderly, single women, and orphans. But seeing this Centre today makes me really believe that dreams do come true.

The visit ended with a presentation from the students reciting poems about Mother's Day and Mother Earth. The BTS delegation sang 'Go Now in Peace' and danced to St. Anne's Reel played by Marcel on his harmonica. We presented the school with a new soccer ball. The students wanted to sing us a few songs after they were encouraged by our presentation. It was great fun being together and a little sad leaving.

For Jeremias, the time at the school was much more emotional.

"I felt so much emotion as I entered the school that day and it felt like a dream," he says. "I was so happy to hear my language, but I was afraid at first to identify myself as one of them. When I did, it brought back my mother and family speaking and joking in my language. It was so good to witness one of the biggest dreams I ever had come true, this school. To actually see that we can make a difference is such a gift. There were 150 kids there; 60 percent travel every day, and 40 percent stay there. They are taught Human Rights, Social Studies, and History, and in the afternoon they learn to farm, grow vegetables, have chickens, pigs and cows and organic herbs. Even traditional customs and medicines are taught. It is so amazing!"

For Jeremias, this was the "shiny day," as he looked forward to seeing the happy children so proud of their Mayan culture. He played soccer with them and listened to their presentations. He also spoke.

"I presented in Achi," he says. "I told them I have the same story as they do. I shared my story and talked about my dream and how I ended up in Canada. I spoke about how our ancestors were with us. They were so surprised. I listened, too, and it touched me. I was happy but sad as they related the bloody story of Rabinal, of the survivors, and those we lost."

As Jeremias talks about this, he becomes quieter and stops talking altogether for a few minutes. As I reach out to give him a reassuring touch, I see the tears.

"Do you want to stop?" I ask in a soft voice. I've come to watch for and respect the limits of the dialogue.

"No, I'm fine," he says with a smile as he continues. "It is just really hard, you know, to go back to a place where you were born and lived as a child, where so many good and bad things happened. It is like a flashlight turning off and on, first good, then bad, then maybe even worse. When I visited the monument with the names of those who died, I could see in my head how some of them died! In was so painful and still so peaceful at the same time."

Jeremias felt sad he could not for safety reasons go to the smaller village o La Ceiba where his home once stood; he went only to the town of Rabinal. He wanted to go, maybe even see Inup again, the tree that saved him and his family, but he could not. It was just too dangerous. He still had aunts and uncles there he knows he will probably never see again. He still feels guilty that he has had such an easy life in Canada, whenever he thinks about the hardships of so many still in Guatemala.

Jeremias wrote in his BTS report of Rabinal: *It is really hard to summarize our bloody history and my part of this story. When we were walking in the cemetery and visiting the various monuments, it was profound to see that there was a place to visit and honour our loved ones. Before, they lay in clandestine graves, which for Mayans create so much pain; for us, it is so important to have a place to connect our spirits with those we have lost. Now, we can bring the marimba, candles, and flowers to their graves to celebrate life, so that our spirits can come together once again.*

Jesús Tecu's explanations throughout our visit were so gentle. He has such a kind and humble spirit, which I respect, and Jesús' struggle for justice is so meaningful and powerful. I know that it isn't easy for survivors of these massacres to talk about it. But at the same time, the sharing of these stories is so important, so that future generations never experience something like this. It is important that younger generations know what truly happened in our communities. **Nunca Más** (*Never again*).

It was also hard to hear about the PACs (Civil Defense Patrols) from the community of Pichec, Rabinal, and how the army tricked innocent people. Members of the community heard gunshots and when they went to report them at the military base, they were accused of being guerrillas, which led to their torture, being marched around the town of Rabinal, and used to instill fear into the population. They were used as an example of what would happen if the army found out that people were guerrillas. My uncles were victims of this massacre, and their names are listed on the monument we visited in Rabinal.

We talk a lot about the various massacres and clandestine cemeteries, but how many people here are still looking for their family members? This was the story of my mom. Until her death, she searched for my two disappeared brothers, during which she was beaten, jailed, and probably sexually abused. Through all those years (1981-99) her hope remained strong. I saw great courage in her as well when I accompanied her on many occasions. She always went to military bases without fear, in search of my brothers, in search of her sons. Rest in peace, Doña Pedrina Quisque Ic. Even though you never found your sons on this earth, you are now reunited with them. Just as we celebrate Mothers' Day in Canada, we celebrate it in Guatemala every year on May 10th to celebrate our courageous and brave mothers, like my mom.

Even though this visit was the day before the official Mother's Day observance, it was also a tribute to Jeremias' brave mother. That day was the darkest and most painful part of his trip. The same day, we all drove north for two hours and took a boat across the lake to the village of Rio Negro where Jesús Tecu was born. The only ones who survived in that place were those who hid in the mountains. It was a place where death still permeated the path up the mountain. For Jeremias, who recalled only too well his own escape through the mountains, the event had a great impact.

"We walked the same path the military forced the martyrs to walk those years before," he says. "We were at six stops that are marked to show where different groups of people lost their lives. It was very humbling. I felt the energy. Sometimes I was numb. I could hear the crying and the pleas for mercy. The children did not even know what was happening. They did not know they were never coming back again. It was too hard to imagine the brutality, the cruelty. I felt responsible and I felt speechless. It's part of my story and I felt our connection. How can we share this to make sure it is not repeated? Too many innocent people died!"

Another BTS delegate, Dave MacPherson, writes about this Pilgrimage to Rio Negro: *What if you lived in a peaceful village on a beautiful river that provided all that you needed— fish to eat and excellent growing conditions on rich bottom land? What if the government said we're going to take your land to give to a large European Corporation to build a dam to provide electricity to large industry? Would you be upset? Would you resist?*

The people of Rio Negro did resist—and were massacred for their resistance as part of the genocide against the indigenous Mayan people. This massacre was carried out by a combined force of Guatemalan Army and Civil Patrol. The Civil Patrol was made up of neighbours forced to do the dirty work of the government. First the men were murdered, as they were accused of supporting the rebels during the civil war. Then 70 women and 107 children of Rio Negro were marched into the mountain high above the village and were humiliated, tortured, raped, and murdered in the most horrific manner imaginable.

I first visited the site of the massacre 10 years ago and was left with a sickening memory of man's dark and godless side. This took place on March 13, 1982. The pilgrimage today was still emotionally difficult, but a bit more positive as some families have returned to their homeland and are practicing their Mayan culture in their ancestral home. During the civil war, between 250,000 and 300,000 Guatemalan citizens were killed, the majority of whom were indigenous Maya. News of the Guatemalan Civil War was virtually non-existent in Canada.

Jeremias explains that 18 children from that time were taken by the soldiers to be servants and one of these was Jesús Tecu. In his book, *Memoir of the Rio Negro Massacres*, published by the BTS Network, Jesús Tecu Osorio describes what happened as he faced death before he was taken to be a servant by the man who slaughtered his baby brother: *My two-year-old brother and I were right in front of the patrollers. With every passing second, I could feel death coming to catch me. The patroller Pedro Gonzalaz called me and said: I am not going to kill you, but you have to come with me to Xococ and help me with my work. I insisted on taking my brother with me, He became angry and said if I persisted, he would kill us both. I was sitting on the trunk of a fallen tree. I had my brother in my arms, but he took him by force. He wrapped a rope around his neck and took him hanging from one of his hands. Jaime was kicking his feet. I followed him crying. I said I was sorry thousands of times, so that he would spare my brother's life, but it did nothing.*

I wished for someone to help me, but no one appeared. We arrived at the ravine where the bodies of the victims were dumped. He threw my brother to the ground. He took him by the feet and smashed him against the rocks. Upon seeing that he was dead he threw him into the ravine. There I could see that the women had been raped, hung, shot, and killed with machetes. Some of the bodies were still trembling.

Jeremias is still overwhelmed when he thinks about the lack of mercy shown to all the innocent people. The memories are so vivid he needs to put an end to the telling of this story. We are sitting in my kitchen, a place where he has been able to allow himself to trust enough to show his vulnerability as he shares these memories.

27

Where to Go from Here

Sometimes the telling of the story is empowering, even though the accounts are those of unbelievable cruelty and injustice, and I can see it in his glowing face and the set of his shoulders: the warrior stance. But when the telling unlocks the flood gates of memories that catapult along with tears and the trembling shoulders of a frightened child, then it is I who must be the safe haven, a caring mother/grandmother, and halt the process. It is important to allow time for silence in this safe space, and a return to stories of the beauty of simple truths, like the resilience of the spider Jeremias admires so much, or the power of a sunrise. We visit those tales often.

He tells me he could not tell this story outside of a safe space, and there have been times when we met elsewhere, that he refused to talk about anything except present-day politics. I respect this and give him time to continue to test the safety of our relationship. I know if I press him for information, I may not talk to him again for months, so I have learned to go with the flow. The re-storying process always needs to be controlled by the storyteller. I am just there to validate the telling. He validates the tale. Therapists need to remember this.

One of the most challenging aspects of the therapeutic process for me in working with marginalized clients who have been traumatized (including newcomers to Canada) has been accepting the fact that my 'best practice' treatment plans are often not best practice for the client, and may need to be changed several times.

In any counselling model, the therapist establishes goals that serve as guidelines for the therapy. There may be adjustments to the goals along the way, but the goals themselves usually remain quite constant. For example, one might begin with a goal of giving the client strategies to cope with stress more effectively. This could easily get tweaked to include establishing a self-care plan; the therapist refers to outside agencies for anything considered outside of mental health therapy. If a client spends a session talking about things that appear unrelated to the therapy or distant from a solution focus, the therapist will usually redirect and ask questions to gently guide the client. For me, this is what I was trained to do, but this does not always work well with clients who are new to the therapeutic process. I was once working with a small group of First Nation survivors from residential school and tried gently redirecting the conversations by inserting a simple question. I had employed this kind of practice many times with success and it had worked well. But I was told on the spot that my redirection was disrespectful.

I knew my intentions were honourable. I thought I was being helpful and supportive by introducing a question I believed would take the participants to an area I considered solution-focused. But the participants saw my question as an indication I did not want to hear their stories. They NEEDED to tell their stories, all of them, and it needed to take as long as they decided it needed to take.

Again, in working with Jeremias, I was reminded time and time again that ALL conversation is relevant to the process, and that my role is most often to just listen. Sometimes remarkable healing comes when I do nothing more than this. Traditional short-term models of counselling (like Employee Assistant Plans or government programs) cannot provide the time needed to see positive results. Relationship/trust-building alone takes several sessions. Survivors of trauma, marginalized peoples, and those who have experienced the challenges associated with the refugee process, need longer-term services that can be offered in a setting that is welcoming and feels safe for them.

Because this kind of model does not fit well into a traditional counselling practice, most of my work with newcomers to Canada, including Jeremias, was *pro bono*, and allowed me to experiment with settings and time periods. Some paid work in First Nations communities allowed me to also experiment on how to best bring services to the communities. In one New Brunswick Mi'kmaq community, I actually set aside two days of open 'office hours' in a building within their Health Centre. Cli-ents could sign up or just drop in to see if a time were available. They could book two-hour spots or just 15 minutes. It was *first come, first served* and it worked well.

Jeremias taught me so much about listening and allowing the storyteller to direct the telling. I learned to constantly adjust my treatment plan to become his treatment plan. And I quickly learned to stop trying to push the process. Sometimes we met weekly and sometimes he needed a three-month break. Again, I learned to go with the flow.

For Jeremias, his last visit to Guatemala cemented his determination to do whatever he could to help people who still live in the dire circumstances there. He left feeling heavy-hearted but decisive in the path he would need to take to do this. For Jeremias, this is about connection—connection between the south and the north, between North America, Canada in particular—and Central America.

"Each country is affected by the other," he says. "We all need to stand up for the healing of Mother Earth. She doesn't need us; we need Her."

In Guatemala, the youth have started a group to stand against mining. In fact, one of the leaders, Topacio Reynoso, (a 16-year-old girl) was shot for her bravery. Her father was also injured.

"They killed our leaders and they thought that would make us be quiet, but it has made us more determined," says Jeremias. "I know what I must do now. Our youth in Canada need to connect with the youth in Guatemala, so we can make the dream come true. The future is in the hands of our youth. They are the change."

Jeremias believes it can start with the south and the north but someday it will be worldwide. He realizes that was one of the reasons he survived and came to Canada. He works with many youth who all want the same thing. They want peace and they want Mother Earth to heal. And for those who are still hurting and need a purpose, he can help them find this way of speaking for peace.

"I can try to inspire the youth and find other supporters," he says with a smile, tears now evaporated like prayers to the heavens. "I can't move an elephant if I am an ant, but many ants can do it. And if I do this thing, then I will rest in peace. I want to tell this story to all classrooms in universities, so they can learn about the truth behind the wars, that even Canada and the United States were part of this, and that it is about big business and greed. I think it is time for our society to be informed, and as a war child I can testify and share my testimony: that in my family's case we were victims of a civil war between two groups, and both groups were killers. I was just a child caught up in their game."

28

Closure?

On Mon, Apr 2, 2018 at 11:45 AM Lisa Rankin, Breaking the Silence Coordinator wrote: *Friends, Efrain Rios Montt, de facto president of Guatemala from March 1982 to August 1983, died yesterday. His legacy as a genocidal dictator was ce-mented in May, 2013, during the Genocide Trial, where he was convicted of genocide against the Maya Ixil people. Although this sentence was overturned ten days later on a procedural appeal, the case continues to stand as a significant moment in Guatemalan history, where a head of state was convicted of genocide.*

On his death, Rios Montt was under house arrest, and in the midst of the repetition of the genocide trial, where witnesses had been testifying against him and his former head of military intelligence, Jose Mauricio Rodriguez Sanchez, since October. Rios Montt both reportedly died and was buried on the same day— an act which exemplifies the family's fear of a public ceremony.

Survivors and family members of the massacred, assassinated, and disappeared, have expressed their indignation that Rios Montt never spent a day in jail, and died before the repeat of the trial was finished. Many of the survivors and witnesses in the case have also died in the slow process of bringing crimes of the past to justice.

A BTS blog posted on December 16, 2019 says:

Hearings on the Maya Ixil genocide case began in early November 2019. On November 4th, the first hearing was held on the case representing 1731 victims against military men Benedicto Lucas Garcia and Manuel Callejas y Callejas on charges of crimes against humanity, genocide, and forced disappearances. Both the accused have already been sentenced in the Molina Theissen case. Among the new charges are those of 42 rapes, 81 forced disappearances, and 404 victims of massacres from 1978-1982 during the presidency of Romero Lucas Garcia. Most of the victims range in age from 0-12 years old.

On November 29th, Judge Jimy Rodolfo Bremer Ramirez also gave the official order to initiate the trial against Colonel Luis Enrique Mendoza Garcia for genocide and crimes against humanity against 1,442 Maya Ixil peoples between April 1982, and July 1983. The case provides sufficient proof that as part of the military coup government of Efrain Rios Montt, Mendoza Garcia was a military leader who participated in cruel and violent treatments by the state against civilian populations. The judge also added that there is reason to believe that there was an intention to eliminate the Maya Ixil population, who were seen as combative and rebellious. Bail for the accused was set at Q30,000 (approximately $5,000 CDN) and he was placed under house arrest, as well as prohibited from traveling outside the department of Guatemala.

29

Jeremias Talks About Services for Survivors of War and Torture

"To tell my story has been so difficult and challenging for me. It is not an easy task. I have to pray, and I have to be patient in order not to feel the pain. I don't want to see my *little me* running from death, but I must if I am to tell it. Not everyone can do this, and it takes time and trust. It took me a long time to trust anyone. It was the idea of telling my story as a way to heal that caught my attention. To hear this from someone who also used storytelling to heal made me start the journey to trust her to help me. She was a therapist, but she was also a person who knew about healing from pain, and she shared some of her story. That helped me trust her.

"I think therapists need to be real people, not just professionals, to those who have been so wounded. I needed something real, someone who can share part of themselves, too, and let me know they understand. I needed to humanize the experience of counselling and therapy. Too many professionals miss this. My process has helped me. I tried so many things before. There are no mental health services that would do it. I don't think they realize how it is for someone like me. By draining my pain slowly through my words and my tears, I see hope for a better life for me and for my children. I can look through more positive eyes and know that everything is possible, that I can cry without being embarrassed, and when I have a hard time I can reach for help.

"There are things that can help with this kind of therapy, to aid the healing. Perhaps it would help to have frequent follow-up. Checking to see how someone is doing could be part of the process. Regular mental health therapists do not do this. When I was working with Eve all these years, she often checked on me through emails and she would send me questions. Sometimes she would text or call, but she soon learned I do not like talking about anything too serious on the phone. It is a matter of trust. Some of the questions were too hard to talk about except in person. I would not respond at all at first, and she would wonder what was wrong. When I told her this, she agreed to only talk about the harder things at her home or mine. When a mental health client opens up and starts sharing painful memories, it is important to check and make sure the talking did not open something that would injure them instead of helping. For me, when I would talk about painful things, we would change and talk about something happy before I left. Even then, the memories stirred up might be with me for days. That is why it was so important to have someone check on me.

"Settings are so important. Not everyone can open up and talk in an office. There has to be a better way. Even walking and talking in a park near a river or sitting at a picnic table could make it easier. I know this might be hard for a therapist, but no newcomer will talk freely about something so terrible sitting in a small office, that might even look like a room where they were once held captive. Today, I get newcomers to open up to me while playing sports or listening to music. It makes them relax more.

"If a professional is tired or uncomfortable, they need to say this. I could tell by his body language when I visited a therapist once that he did not seem to be really listening to me, but I could not understand why. He was quick to tell me when the time was up, and I was glad to leave. Telling this kind of story cannot always go on scheduled time limits. Maybe in the beginning I can only talk for 10 minutes. When I get to a point that I open up and go so deep and I give my all, then I need time, my time, not a set time limit of 50 minutes where the therapist or psychologist keeps looking at his or her watch. I don't know how this can be done, but it is the only way it will work.

"There is also an issue about the cost. Newcomers with severe PTSD cannot be cured in five or six 50-minute sessions, and most cannot afford ongoing therapy. The wait list for mental health services is too long and too regulated to allow trust to develop. Maybe a counsellor who is available for a day or two on a site where the client feels safer and could book their own length of time might work. There should be no judging. The therapist needs to accept the importance of our spiritual and traditional beliefs, even if they might not believe the same way. If they listen, we will tell you why this is important. One good thing for me in this process, I always knew my therapist/writer/friend was listening.

"It takes courage to share all this painful history. We need to know that it is respected. For me, when I hear too much injustice in the world or when I hear about war, negative memories come to my mind. It is a trigger that some might not experience. I cannot tolerate any violation of human rights. It makes me sad and upset. That is where I think my courage is coming from, because I wish to contribute to our society and hope for a free world. If I want a better world, I have to contribute! I want to share this story although I know it is so bloody, but in this blood, I see *hope*; I see a wonderful seed of happiness and of course forgiveness. We have to come to a place where we choose to forgive, to release ourselves from it. Then we are free."

30

From the Therapist/Writer/Friend of Jeremias Tecu

In 2017, I attended a two-day workshop in Moncton, New Brunswick, Canada: *Refugees and Trauma: Understanding and Supporting Resilience*, provided by the Crisis & Trauma Institute. It talked about all the important factors concerning the treatment of PTSD for those who come to a new country through the refugee experience, and one of the topics focused on supporting recovery after trauma.

It was a great learning experience, and I certainly walked away with new ideas and techniques that I thought I might find helpful. I valued the words of wisdom and experience I heard from others in attendance. I also walked away saddened by the truth that the support so desperately needed by all the men, women and children coming from war-torn countries to a new world, hoping to find peace (including peace of mind), could never be a reality within the current framework of mental health services.

Perhaps the establishment of *healing centres* for newcomers, with a mental health team that allow therapists to see clients in various settings on a drop-in basis, funded by the federal government as part of their after-care, might be a start. Using participatory art, games, music, dance, sports, or storytelling to augment current modalities of practice must become more the norm than an occasional "go to." One size of counselling does not fit all, or even most. Each individual needs a tailor-made approach. That means learning humbly, open to being taught, regardless of years of experience or expertise, how to sit with the client, as I needed to learn with Jeremias.

I started my relationship with Jeremias as a writer with a mental health background, hoping to share some creative writing tips that might also have therapeutic benefits. I did not expect to be his therapist. I never considered myself to actually be his therapist at any time, but rather a friend who needed to use my therapeutic knowledge and experience to help him as he told his story—a bit like a midwife helping with the birthing process. We both seemed to know intuitively what the boundaries were.

Jeremias was one child profoundly affected by war and torture. To say his own resilience aided his survival would be an understatement. Therapists need to be open to exploring the spiritual possibilities in treatment as the client leads. To attribute Jeremias' survival to a divine Higher Power, God, would be a truth perhaps debated by many, but not by Jeremias, and *he* is the expert in his own story. He did survive, but he did not find here in his new home the help he needed to cope with the anguish in his mind and spirit, the torment that did not stay in Guatemala when his body arrived safely in Canada. Today, many refugees arrive with the same mental health needs. Their stories need to be told, and the telling validated, so they can heal.

Telling his story helped Jeremias, and it will help others. We all have our own truths; everyone has a story. Not all stories need to be written or published in books, but all must be told. They must be told to someone who truly listens and validates the storyteller, someone the teller can trust, and in an environment where they feel safe. As Maya Angelou, American poet, singer, memoirist, and civil rights activist, once said: *"There is no greater burden than carrying an untold story."*

On January 12, 2020, Jeremias' father, Don Felix Tecu, passed over to the spirit world. He was celebrated and buried in Rabinal BV. Jeremias was not able to attend, but he finds comfort knowing his father will now be safe in his beloved country and forever sheltered in the arms of Inup.

Funeral Observance for his Father at Jeremias' Home

Bibliography

REMHI, Recovery of Historical Memory Project: the official report of the Human Rights Office, Archdiocese of Guatemala. (1999). *Guatemala, never again!* Maryknoll, NY. London: Orbis Books; CIIR: Latin America Bureau (3, 77, 156).

BTS blog: http://www.breakingthesilenceblog.com

Rothenberg, D., & Comisión para el Esclarecimiento Histórico (Guatemala). (2012). *Memory of silence: The Guatemalan Truth Commission Report*. New York: Palgrave Macmillan (220).

Sanford, V. (2003). *Buried secrets: Truth and human rights in Guatemala*. New York: Palgrave Macmillan (17, 18, 38).

Upside Down World News: http://upsidedownworld.org

New Hope Foundation—La Fundación Nueva Esperanza, available at http://www.fne.cosmosmaya.info/bienvenidos en.html

Río Negro Massacres v. Guatemala, Inter-American Court of Human Rights (IACrtHR), 4 September 2012, available at: https://www.refworld.org/cases,IACRTHR,564ed2714.html

Osorio, Jesus Tecu (2012). *Memoir of the Rio Negro Massacres*. Translated from the Spanish & published with assistance of Rights Action & Breaking the Silence Solidarity Network, available at:Tatamagouche Centre - Contact kathrynande@gmail.com (85, 87, 88 & 181).

Acknowledgements

I am so grateful for all the life-changing lessons I learned from my friendship with Jeremias Tecu and his son Oscar. This process of storytelling impacted all of us and I applaud Jeremias and Oscar for having the courage to speak their truth.

Brazilian author Paulo Coelho says: "Tears are words that need to be written." There were certainly many tears, as well as smiles, during the creation of this book, and in the writing of it, healing was given its space to grow. This I believe was the purpose all along. Our meeting was very much a serendipitous event. Gracias, mi amigo Jeremias! Gracias, mi amigo Oscar!

I would also like to thank my son, Jody Claus, who lives in Fredericton, New Brunswick, for his patience in creating the artwork for the cover of this book. He is a Mohawk artist and his creations have appeared in the *Nashwaak Review* and in my first book, *Little White Squaw: A White Woman's Story of Abuse, Addiction and Reconciliation* (coauthored with Kenneth J. Harvey), as well as in publications for local organizations and fundraising events.

In the early draft stages of my manuscript there were two friends who eagerly proofread for me and encouraged my efforts. Thank you, Nancy George and Clinton Matchett, for your help and Ian Heft for your help with the final edit. Thank you also to my friend and fellow writer, Rose Burke, for your reinforcement throughout this journey. Thank you to my granddaughter, Sasha Laagland, who photographed me for this book, as she did for my first book back in 2002.

Thank you to Sandra Devink, Helen Massfeller and Suzanne Dudziak for guidance, encouragement, and your gracious endorsements. Thank you to my mentor and friend, Kenneth J. Harvey, for the kind words and advice throughout the years. Gracias, Valarie Kilfoil, for the unexpected photos from Guatemala.

I want to acknowledge the valuable contribution of BTS throughout the years. Their vigorous efforts made a significant difference in the lives of many Guatemalans, including those of Jeremias and his family. They are an important part of this story, and definitely part of the solution when it comes to helping survivors find healing.

Finally, I want to thank the Multicultural Associations throughout Canada and in particular the Multicultural Association of Fredericton (MCAF), who work incessantly without all the resources required to adequately meet the needs of newcomers to Canada, helping them settle and find a new beginning. It was at the MCAF that I met Jeremias and began a new journey of healing and discovery with him. As a result, our authentic inner storytellers crafted this book, written in remembrance of all those who never had the opportunity to tell their stories. In this way, we honour all those who have died. Their spirit and example will remain with us forever. *Presente*.

Eve Mills Allen MA MEd LCT CCC

Oscar Tecu
Chillteens Band, Fredericton, New Brunswick

Photo Credit: Sara Hellingwerf

This is an intimate portrait of a survivor of the Guatemalan genocide against Mayan peoples. With courage and determination, Jeremias, the hero of the story, breaks the silence that is causing him immense internal suffering. He reveals his memories to the book's author in a profoundly moving process spread over several years. We learn how totally inadequate our mental health system is to offer true healing to those traumatized by war and genocide. In turn, the author shares her own experience as counsellor/friend in writing Jeremias's story.

Breaking the silence can still mean the difference between life and death. This book tells of the horrors of the genocide, and of the spiritual and cultural practices that sustain survivors. We come to understand that the only answer to collective trauma is to finally halt 'la violencia.' In receiving this story, we readers share in this responsibility.

www.ingramcontent.com/pod-product-compliance
Lightning Source LLC
Chambersburg PA
CBHW051545010526
44118CB00022B/2583